"HAVE I COMMITTED THE UNPARDONABLE SIN?"

And Other Questions You've Wanted to Ask About the Christian Faith

C. Donald Cole

Crossway Books • Westchester, Illinois
A Division of Good News Publishers

Biblical quotations are taken from the *New International Version,* unless otherwise indicated.

"Have I Committed the Unpardonable Sin?" Copyright © 1984 by C. Donald Cole. Published by Crossway Books, a division of Good News Publishers, Westchester, Illinois 60153.

Cover design by Lane T. Dennis

First printing, 1984

Printed in the United States of America

Library of Congress Catalog Card Number 84-71421

ISBN 0-89107-317-5

CONTENTS

The Lord is my shepherd, I shall lack nothing. (Psalm 23:1)

Look at the birds of the air; they do not sow or reap or store away in barns, and yet our heavenly Father feeds them. Are you not much more valuable than they? (Matthew 6:26)

God is love. (1 John 4:16)

But God demonstrates his own love for us in this: While we were still sinners, Christ died for us. (Romans 5:8)

1/DOES GOD CARE WHAT HAPPENS TO ME?

We have all heard that God loves us. But does he, really? Then why is life so difficult? If God cares, why doesn't he make things easier?

Does God care about me?

Of course he does! That's what the Bible is all about—telling us that God loves us and cares very much what happens to us. The Apostle John said that "God is love," then explained his statement in these words: "This is how God showed his love among us: He sent his one and only Son into the world that we might live through him" (1 John 4:9). That means that God doesn't just talk about his love for us; he proves it.

The greatest proof is in the gift of his Son. The Bible says, "God so loved the world that he gave his one and only Son, that whoever believes in him shall not perish but have eternal life" (John 3:16). Another apostle, Paul, explained that since God did not spare his own Son, but gave him up for us all, there is nothing he will not give us (see Romans 8:32). Having given us his best gift, he will not withhold lesser gifts.

Lesser gifts include material things and the ability to laugh and rejoice. The Apostle Paul told the citizens of an ancient town in what is now Turkey that God "has shown kindness by giving (us) rain from heaven and crops in their season; he provides (us) with plenty of food and fills (our) hearts with joy" (Acts 14:17). All these things are evidence of his concern for us—for our bodies and souls alike.

It troubles him (if you'll permit the expression) when we suffer want because we have plundered this planet. Hunger was never God's will for mankind; it became a fact of life through our despoliation of the earth. We turned his gardens into deserts; we dried up streams flowing with sweet water and abounding in fish. Now we suffer the consequences in widespread hunger and, in some cases, thirst. But this was never God's plan.

Even so, he cares for us. In a world made sad by sin, even holy people have their share of griefs and sorrows. But God does care; he has said so. And the testimony of men and women of God confirms it.

Does God have a blueprint for my life?

Does God have special designs for your life? Well, the testimony of certain persons in the Bible is that he does. A great Christian of the first century, Paul, said he was "an apostle of Christ Jesus by the will of God" (1 Corinthians 1:1). On one occasion he said, "God . . . always leads us in triumphal procession in Christ" (2 Corinthians 2:14). He also spoke of his desire to spend some time with his friends as if the visit were contingent upon the will of God. "I hope to spend some time with you," he said, "if the Lord permits" (1 Corinthians 16:7).

Then there was David, king of Israel, and as such free to do what he pleased, you might think. Yet he expressed his need of and confidence in God's guidance. Here's what he said in prayer: "You hold me by my right hand. You guide me with your counsel, and afterward you will take me into glory" (Psalm 73:23, 24). And it was probably David's son, Solomon, who wrote the words of Proverbs 3, so familiar to many of us: "Trust in the Lord with all your heart and lean not on your own understanding; in all your ways acknowledge him, and he will make your paths straight" (verses 5, 6).

Now the thrust of these passages, and many others that could be quoted, is that a true believer is not left to figure things out for himself. He is not like a carpenter with a keg of nails and a truckload of studs, but no blueprint. God has told us the kind of life he wants us to build. Our Lord said that he came that men might have life "in all its fullness" (John 10:10, NEB). God is not pleased with lives out of plumb, like a house built without plans.

Straight lines and square corners are possible only in lives lived according to God's instructions. These are found in the Bible; the Bible gives the blueprint. The plan begins with a genuine conversion experience and proceeds to show us what to avoid, and what to do. Not included are trivial matters, such as the color of your wallpaper. God's plan is not concerned with anything that does not contribute in some way to the building of Christian character and the proclamation of his Word.

So nobody should think that the idea of a divine plan for our lives short-circuits our brains, or relieves us of responsibility for thinking and making decisions. The Bible tells us what kind of life God wants us to live; it gives us a set of values whereby we may measure every stick we knock into the framework of our lives. But it doesn't do our thinking for us, and doesn't do the choosing.

Obviously, anyone can ignore the plans. And that's bad news, especially in the case of those who don't even lay a foundation according to God's Word. Since the foundation is Jesus Christ—i.e., a personal relationship with him—to fail here is to lose your soul. Nothing could be more dreadful.

Why doesn't God do something about the pain and suffering in the world?

This is a curious question for a world that largely ignores God, since the question implies the existence of a Being able—if only willing—to do something about pain. Everybody knows we are so constructed that pain is sometimes unavoidable. Our nerve endings screech in protest when our bodies are injured. But we humans aren't the only creatures to suffer; all life forms seem to suffer pain or even to cause pain—as in the case of predators which exist by destroying other creatures. With us, however, pain may be intensified by our ability to anticipate it and to question it. Why *should* we suffer? we moan, scarcely realizing that what we are really asking is why a God who is supposedly all-good and all-powerful doesn't do anything about pain.

The answer may be that God can't completely eliminate pain. This doesn't mean that God is not all-powerful, since he surely is. Yet there are some things he cannot do. For instance, he cannot deny himself (2 Timothy 2:13), and he cannot be tempted with evil (James 1:13). Thus, it's not strictly correct to say that God can do anything.

Applied to the question at hand, this may mean that God cannot give us both freedom of choice and freedom from pain. The world in which we live has fixed laws which if violated—as well they may be by free agents—exact a penalty. If men exercising their freedom of choice choose to fight each other, they must take the consequences. A nose that intercepts a fast-moving fist inevitably suffers pain. Such is the nature of matter.

Remember, God did not invent pain and suffering, nor is he indifferent to it. If he were, he would not have commanded us to alleviate it, or commended the good Samaritan for having poured oil on the wounds of the man who was mugged on the way to Jericho. Pain and suffering are not intrinsically good; in themselves, they are evil.

Nevertheless, God uses pain. Kathryn Lindskoog summarized C. S. Lewis's view of suffering: "Pain is the megaphone which makes evil impossible to ignore. . . . Pain shatters the illusion that all is well; then pain shatters the illusion that what we have is our own and enough for us. Pain can lead an unbeliever to religion and to God; it can force a Christian to depend upon God as he should" (in *C. S. Lewis: Mere Christian,* page 154).

A passage in Hebrews 12 confirms this by speaking of pain and suffering in terms of discipline. Discipline has definite values; the least that can be said is that it is evidence—in some cases—of a relationship with God. Furthermore, it does a job in a Christian's heart. As the Bible says, "To those who have been trained by it . . . it produces a harvest of righteousness and peace" (Hebrews 12:11). If there were no other reason for the continued existence of pain and suffering in the world, that one alone would suffice.

You see, the possibility of evil (and the suffering it causes) is inherent in freedom. Humanly speaking, God took a chance when he made us in his own image and likeness. Whatever his image means, it surely includes rational thought, freedom of choice, and an essentially moral nature. Unlike beasts, we are responsible for what we do. We do not act according to inexorable laws of instinct; in meaningful situations we have alternatives, we have choices. The rub is, we must often choose between good and evil. Where good is present, its alternative—evil—also exists.

We find choosing evil easier than choosing good. The explanation is that we are fallen creatures with a proneness to do wrong. Some schools of thought reject this view, of course; they prefer to regard man as an evolving life form as yet imperfectly developed. For us Christians, it is hard to take such theories seriously. First, they do violence to Scripture. Second, they don't really make sense; they do not account for scientific data, nor do they explain the gap between intellectual and moral development. They can't even explain the fact of moral concepts. How can an uncreated thing, an evolving life form, even think in terms of good and evil?

The biblical explanation alone makes sense and jibes with the facts of human history. As Paul explains, "Sin entered the world through one man (Adam) and . . . all sinned" (Romans 5:12). The Bible describes us as sinners by nature as well as in deed. Thus, God himself had (and has) only three alternatives in the face of sin: to wipe us out and thereby cleanse his universe; to accept evil as inevitable; or to do what he has in fact done.

What has he done? He has done two things. First, through the incarnation, death, resurrection, and ascension of Christ, he has made it possible for himself to forgive sin without compromising his holiness. Second, he has set a date for terminating sin in the universe. Peter says God has "set a day" when he will put an end to all sinning and begin all over again with a new heavens and a new earth, "the home of righteousness" (Acts 17:31; 2 Peter 3:13).

Meanwhile, evil is restrained. Satan is active, to be sure. He is the archenemy, the deceiver of mankind, an evil personage to which there are many references in the Bible. But he is on a leash; he may rampage and he may cause innumerable sorrows in the world, but his power is limited (2 Thessalonians 2:6, 7). Not only so, but he is doomed—which is one aspect of the blessed hope enjoyed by Christians who know their Bibles. As Martin Luther's great hymn has it: "The prince of darkness grim / We tremble not for him; / His rage we can endure, / For lo, his doom is sure, / One little word shall fell him. . . ." Paul says, "The God of peace will soon crush Satan under your feet" (Romans 16:20).

When that day comes, the world will know that God has always been in control. The world will also know what it does not now know: *why* God permitted the activity of Satan and the sinful works of men and women. Meanwhile, like Abraham, we trust the Judge of all the earth to do what is right (cf. Genesis 18:25).

All have sinned and fall short of the glory of God, and are justified freely by his grace through the redemption that came by Jesus Christ. (Romans 3:23, 24)

Jesus said . . . "I have come that they may have life, and have it to the full." (John 10:7, 10)

At that time Jesus said, . . . "Come to me, all you who are weary and burdened, and I will give you rest." (Matthew 11:25, 28)

To all who received him, to those who believed in his name, he gave the right to become children of God. (John 1:12)

2/WHY IS LIFE SO FLAWED? HOW CAN I MAKE MY LIFE HAPPIER OR BETTER?

Sometimes the stress and strain of life make us wonder what the reason for it all is. What direction should our lives be taking, and how do we get there?

Does God hold us responsible for what we do?

Yes, he does. There is a major passage on this subject in Paul's Epistle to the Romans. It begins by saying, "The wrath of God is being revealed from heaven against all the godlessness and wickedness of men who suppress the truth by their wickedness," and it ends with an important statement about personal responsibility: "Now we know that whatever the law says, it says to those who are under the law, so that every mouth may be silenced and the whole world held accountable to God" (Romans 1:18; 3:19).

Two kinds of offenders are in mind: the gross sinner whom everybody condemns, and the cultured, religious type who glories in his supposed superiority. Before God there's no difference—not, at least, in this respect, that both kinds are personally responsible for what they do. "Held accountable"—those are the words Paul uses, and nobody can fail to grasp their meaning—God holds people responsible for what they do.

It should be understood, of course, that the passage cited is by no means the only statement on the subject. In fact, personal responsibility is one of the major themes of the Bible. It gives force to the gospel, because there would be no need of a gospel if people weren't lost and doomed by a God who sees all and excuses nothing (see Exodus 34:7, for example). The Old Testament has plenty to say about God's judging the world (see the Psalms), and the New Testament confirms it. Our Lord himself pronounced woe upon certain kinds of sinners, and in a well-known parable of sheep and goats he described a judgment yet to come when men and women will be divided into two groups. Some will be eternally lost, others saved. Where they spend eternity will be determined by a person's individual worth and his response to Christ; personal responsibility for one's actions—that is the great lesson.

Our Lord frequently spoke about personal responsibility. When he said "If your right eye causes you to sin, gouge it out and throw it away," he used a singular pronoun. "You," singular, and "your" eye. Then he said, "It is better for you (singular) to lose one part of your body than for your whole body to go into hell" (Matthew 5:29, 30).

Paul stressed personal responsibility. He bawled out certain Christians for criticizing others and told them, in effect, to mind their own business. Why? Because Christ is Lord and therefore judge. Then Paul said, "We will all stand before God's judgment seat," and he quoted an Old Testament passage where it says that "every knee will bow before [the Lord]," and "every tongue will confess to God" (Romans 14:9-11).

It would be easy to go through the Bible and find great statements about personal responsibility for one's conduct. They are all weighty and solemn, and none more so than those in the last chapter of the Bible. Again, the warnings are directed to individuals: God holds everybody responsible for what he or she does, and eternal destiny is at stake.

There are schools of thought that teach people to shift responsibility for their failings to others. They're quite clever about it. But at judgment time nobody will get by with that; we will not be able to blame anybody for what we have done. Because God sent his Son to be our Savior, no excuses will be acceptable from those who refused to receive him. It's scary to think about this, and it should be.

Are people basically good or basically evil?

In one of his speeches made while campaigning for the Presidency in 1952, Adlai Stevenson promised to talk sense to the American people and to tell them the truth. He lost the election, but no one can say he didn't tell them the truth. Take that speech delivered in Hartford when he said, "Nature is neutral. Man has wrested from nature the power to make the world a desert or to make the deserts bloom. There is no evil in the atom; only in men's souls."

There's nothing wrong with that statement, but it doesn't go far enough. That evil festers and schemes in the human soul has been admitted by every thoughtful person. The writer Joseph Conrad said, "The belief in a supernatural source of evil is not necessary; men alone are quite capable of every wickedness" *(Under Western Eyes)*.

Both Adlai Stevenson and Joseph Conrad acknowledged human potential for evil. But the rub is, they may have failed to see that people are *essentially* evil, not just capable of evil. A popular approach sees man as an imperfect product of evolution, as if his brain had evolved faster and truer than his soul. In time, the theory claims, the problem will solve itself, if mankind can be prevented from destroying itself before evil is eradicated. This view of man is incorrect according to the Bible. The Bible teaches that people are basically evil.

This does not mean that everyone is as bad as he can be, or that nobody is any good. It simply means that people are flawed by sin, with the effect that it is infinitely easier for all of us to sin than to do what is right. The wrong choice is nearly always, if not always, the easier choice.

The prophet Jeremiah expressed it neatly when he said that "the heart" of man, meaning the central part of his personality, "is deceitful above all things and beyond cure" (Jeremiah 17:9). "Who can understand it?" he asked. Ancient Israel's King David said, "Surely I have been a sinner from birth, sinful from the time my mother conceived me" (Psalm 51:5). He did not mean that his mother sinned in bearing him; he meant simply that he was basically evil from the moment of conception.

The testimony of truly good men is always similar to that of

Jeremiah and David. They know their innate capacity for evil; by measuring themselves against the standards of the Bible they know that resistance to evil is a lifelong, sometimes losing battle. For those who don't resist the evil in them, it's no struggle at all, of course, though they also may chafe under certain restraints imposed from without, such as the strong arm of the law.

God's point of view is decidedly more emphatic than ours. We may admit to sin in ourselves, but he assures us that we don't know the half. From his point of view—that is, from the standpoint of an infinitely holy God—we are utterly sinful. The Apostle Paul explains this exceeding sinfulness in various terms. He says that we were "dead in [our] transgressions and sins" (Ephesians 2:1). We were (*were,* that is, in the case of those who have been changed by the grace of God) "by nature objects of wrath." We were guilty sinners before God.

The beauty of the Bible's statements about this subject is that they move on to forgiveness and cleansing. God has not left us to wallow in filth or to plot endlessly evil devices. He offers us the opportunity to repent and to believe the good news about his Son, Jesus Christ. The essence of the good news is God's offer not only of forgiveness for what we have done, but renewal. Those who receive Jesus Christ into their hearts become new people, what the Bible calls "God's workmanship, created in Christ Jesus to do good works" (Ephesians 2:10). Not only so, but we "are being transformed into (Christ's) likeness" (2 Corinthians 3:18); perfect likeness to him is our ultimate destiny. God's new humans will be as sinless as nature. But unlike nature, which—as Adlai Stevenson said—is neutral, we shall be holy. No longer evil, not neutral, but essentially and wholly good. What a future for all who belong to Christ.

Is man, being so sinful, absolutely without hope?

A good novelist knows how to expose human foibles and failings; in fact, it is his stock-in-trade. No matter how fine the characterization or plot or prose, in these times a book is a flop if it fails to portray accurately what is commonly called "the human condition."

Maybe this is why so many modern books reflect a kind of despair about the human race, as if men were so hopelessly evil that there is, in fact, no hope.

That's not the biblical point of view. In the Bible there is no dark or tragic vision of man. True, the Bible is never sentimental about the race; its portrayal of the "human condition" is devastatingly accurate. Take this passage from Paul's epistle to the Ephesians: "you were dead in your transgressions and sins . . . you followed the ways of the world and of . . . the spirit who is now at work in those who are disobedient. All of us also lived among them at one time, gratifying the cravings of our sinful nature and following its desires and thoughts. Like the rest, we were by nature objects of wrath" (Ephesians 2:1-3).

No sentiment there. No tragic vision, either. Paul did not merely expose mankind's sinfulness, then recommend resignation, or perhaps suicide. Instead, he spoke of God's love and mercy. "Because of his great love for us," Paul exulted, "God, who is rich in mercy, made us alive with Christ even when we were dead in transgressions—it is by grace you have been saved" (verses 4, 5). Then Paul explained that God has great plans for us: he has given us a place with Christ in the heavenly realms "in order that in the coming ages he might show the incomparable riches of his grace, expressed in his kindness to us in Christ Jesus."

This boggles the mind; it is utterly different from the picture of mankind drawn by the world's great thinkers and writers. Instead of merely describing sin in lurid detail, the Bible tells what sin is and what it does to people—from God's point of view. What writers may think, is of no importance; what God thinks, is a matter of life and death—literally.

Sin takes many forms, but it is always—in its essence—disobedience. It destroys people, bringing them under the judgment of God. But the vision Paul saw was not a vision of inexorable doom; it was a vision of salvation. In Christ—which means in association with him, united to him, which union is accomplished through faith—we have redemption through his blood, the forgiveness of sins, an experience of the riches of God's grace, and even advance knowledge of the plan of God which he will put into effect at the scheduled time (cf. Ephesians 1:7-10).

That's the vision, or at least a small part of it, and as said already, it boggles the mind. Not only so, it lifts a burden from every heart that learns about it, driving out despair and bringing in joy and gladness.

How bad does a person have to be before he becomes a sinner?

Not bad at all! Even very good people are sinners. But a statement like that doesn't make sense unless we know what we mean by the term *sinner* and say where we get our authority for the definition. Taking these things in reverse order, the authority to which I refer is the Bible. If you cannot believe that the Bible is the Word of God, you may not agree with the statement that even good people are sinners. But if you acknowledge the authority of the Bible, then you have to pay attention to what it says.

What does it say? It says, "All have sinned" (Romans 3:23). No accusation could be more all-inclusive than that; nobody is excluded. The Bible says it in more than one way, too. For example: "Now we know that whatever the law says, it says to those who are under the law, so that every mouth may be silenced and the whole world held accountable to God" (Romans 3:19). Or take this analysis of the human condition: "All have turned away, they have together become worthless; there is no one who does good, not even one" (Romans 3:12).

The point of view is God's, of course. By his standards there is no such thing as a truly good person. Measured by purely human standards, some people are very good indeed, certainly a lot better than the world's thieves or pimps or murderers. But even the best of men and women are flawed creatures. The finest human specimen is still a sinner in God's estimate, and if he wants to survive—i.e., spend eternity with God rather than suffer eternal banishment in Hell—he must be forgiven his sins.

There is forgiveness, and this is the great truth that the Bible proclaims. Even without a Bible, most people discover sooner or later that they are sinners. The literature of the world is full of it. The Bible's distinctive contribution to the subject is the sobering truth that God holds us accountable and will bring us into judgment for our sins. But he'd rather forgive us, and he *can* forgive us without compromising his own holiness. This is the great message of the Bible. As the Apostle Paul puts it, God was in Christ reconciling the world to himself (2 Corinthians 5:19). We Christians, Paul explains, are God's ambassadors, as though God were making an appeal to the world through us: "Be reconciled to God! Let God change you from enemies into friends!"

One last word: there is a second sense in which the Bible uses the word *sinner.* It is applied to sinners who refuse forgiveness. Thus, a sinner is a sinner who wants to keep on being a sinner (see Hebrews 12:3; 1 Peter 4:18). There is no hope for people like that, but only "a fearful expectation of judgment" (Hebrews 10:27). I hope you're not that kind of sinner.

What is sin?

It would be hard to improve on the answer given in the *Shorter Catechism:* "Sin is any want of conformity unto, or transgression of, the law of God." The scriptural basis for that concise definition is 1 John 3:4, which reads as follows: "everyone who sins breaks the law; in fact, sin is lawlessness." The law in question is, of course, God's law—i.e., the rule given to us for all our actions. Nonconformity to that law is sin, which may be committed either by doing what we are told not to do, or by failing to do what we should do (James 4:17). In other words, sins of commission and sins of omission.

Actually, there are various aspects of sin. In a single verse in Exodus (34:7), three distinct words are used: "iniquity," "transgression," and "sin" (or in the NIV, "wickedness," "rebellion," and "sin"). In David's confession of his awful sin (Psalm 51), he uses even more words: he speaks of his transgression, his sin, his iniquity, his deceit, and his guilt. He even describes himself—or others like himself—as wicked. David felt that his awful deed combined virtually every aspect of sin.

There are subtle differences in the terms given. *Transgression* is to go beyond the commandment, to violate a known law. *Iniquity* is gross wickedness or injustice. *Deceit*—well, everybody knows what that means. The sinfulness of sin—no matter how it may be described, no matter which of several aspects may be under consideration—lies in the fact that it is an affront to God. It is his laws that are transgressed, his character that is affronted. And since God is love, sin is essentially—on a purely human level—a form of love's opposite: egotism and selfishness and hatred. But at its deepest level, it is hostility toward God.

In Romans 3:23 Paul uses two verbs to define the human condition. The first is a special Greek tense, roughly equivalent to the past tense in English. "For all sinned." That's how it should be translated. Obviously, Paul had in mind the Garden of Eden and the sin committed by Adam and Eve. His point was that all of Adam's descendants—including you and me—were morally involved in that first sin, even though it took place thousands of years before your birth or mine.

The second verb is different; it doesn't describe an action done once for all. Instead, it describes a permanent state. "For all have sinned and *fall short* of the glory of God." The phrase "fall short," with the words that follow, tell what happened as a result of that first sin. Original sin, as theologians sometimes term it, may have been an isolated act in history. Isolated in the sense that it happened once upon a time. But its effects were lasting. The verse, then, could be translated quite freely in this way: "For all sinned and ever since fall short of the glory of God." Falling short is a chronic state; it is the most significant fact of the human experience.

Falling short of what? That's the question. More than one answer is possible. It can mean failure to win God's approval (cf. John 12:43). Or it can mean that man never measures up to the ideal God had in mind when he made man in his own image and likeness (cf. Isaiah 43:7). Or it may mean that by his guilty sinfulness man is disqualified from standing in the presence of God to hear a message from him. Maybe all these concepts are included in the expression, "and fall short of the glory of God."

Two comments are in order. First, everybody falls short. Some persons may be immensely better than others; they know the meaning of self-restraint. And yet, even they fall short of the ideal. A miss, the old saying goes, is as good as a mile. Falling short by half an inch is as much a miss as if it were by a mile. Or, to change the illustration, men in prison are different from each other. Some are lifers, whereas others are in for a short stretch. But in this they are all alike: they are all guilty. All failed to meet the standards imposed by the law of the land. In the same way, those who fancy themselves nice people are equally guilty with the world's worst hoodlums. They all fall short of God's glory.

The second point is that God is determined to repair the damage done by sin. All sinned, to be sure. Indisputably, all fall short of the glory of God. Yet Christ assumed responsibility for the sin of the world. A man named John once pointed a bony finger at Jesus and shouted, "Look, the Lamb of God, who takes away the sin of the world!" (John 1:29). Later, one of the friends of Jesus wrote about him: "He himself bore our sins in his body on the tree" (1 Peter 2:24). The friend's name was Peter, and he knew that Jesus had died to cancel the effects of that original sin committed by Adam.

Not only that, but the glory of God is no longer unattainable. There's a great statement in Romans 5:2; through our Lord Jesus Christ, it says, "we rejoice in the hope of the glory of God." Whatever was lost by Adam's sin was recovered by the obedience of Jesus Christ—his obedience, that is, unto death. We guilty sinners may be forgiven and brought back to God. Did we forfeit his approval? Now we may have it again. Was the image of God in us effaced? Now it is being restored. As the Apostle Paul wrote, "we, who with unveiled faces all reflect the Lord's glory, are being transformed into his likeness with ever-increasing glory, which comes from the Lord, who is the Spirit" (2 Corinthians 3:18).

The seriousness of sin is seen in the fact that it will take a person to Hell. The Apostle Paul said that at our Lord's return, he will deal out retribution to those who do not know God and do not obey his gospel (2 Thessalonians 1:7ff.). Sin has severe consequences; yet, God is willing to fully forgive all who come to him through his Son.

Have I committed the unpardonable sin?

In one of Nathaniel Hawthorne's novels the hero, Ethan Brand, was asked the question, "What is the Unpardonable Sin?" "It is a sin that grew within my breast," replied Ethan Brand. "The sin of an intellect that triumphed over the sense of brotherhood with man and reverence for God." Is *that* the unpardonable sin? Is it intellectual pride? Hawthorne apparently thought so, but what does the Bible designate as the unpardonable sin?

We read in Matthew 12:31, 32 that our Lord said that whoever speaks or blasphemes against the Holy Spirit will *never* be forgiven, neither in this age nor in the age to come (cf. Mark 3:28-30). That was strong language, but the occasion demanded it. Christ had just healed a demoniac, and he overheard his enemies muttering that he was in league with the Devil. "It is only by Beelzebub, the prince of demons, that this fellow casts out demons," they said. He answered them, and it is here, in his reply to those who said his act of healing was through the power of Satan, that we have the words about blasphemy against the Holy Spirit.

The circumstances of the sin should be noted carefully. The Pharisees had seen Jesus perform an obviously supernatural work; he had healed a speechless, blind man. Furthermore, he had freed the man from the power of Satan. Thus, the miracle was unquestionably the work of the Spirit of God. Nevertheless, in the teeth of the evidence, the Pharisees said Jesus was in league with the Devil. They knew better, yet willfully and maliciously ascribed to Satan what was obviously a work of God. The Lord knew what they were thinking. In fact, before Matthew records the Lord's words, he notes that Jesus knew what they were thinking (verse 25). Knowing their thoughts, he said to them what he said. Their sin was deliberate, a conscious, willful rejection of Christ whom they knew to be filled with the Spirit of God.

The question arises, is this sin possible today? In my judgment, no. Christ is no longer here in the flesh. It is by no means as easy to be sure of the source of alleged miracles as it was when he was on earth. Then men could know positively that the work was the power of God; now it isn't always clear. An observer of what others call the work of God may quite sincerely understand a conversion, say, in terms of psychology. Unbelief may be genuinely intellectual. One may even blaspheme the name of Christ ignorantly in unbelief, as did Saul of Tarsus (1 Timothy 1:13) and be forgiven. So it is no longer possible to commit that particular sin condemned by Jesus.

This should be of comfort to those who pray many years for loved ones who do not respond to the gospel. God never gets fed up, never turns away in impatience. But it should not be of comfort to an unsaved person. It may not be possible to commit blasphemy against the Holy Spirit, but unrelenting resistance to him is just as bad. Keep it up until death and the effect will be the same—eternal darkness. In fact, rejection of Christ's gospel, the sin of unbelief, will be unpardonable in the afterlife.

In his conversation with Nicodemus (John 3) Jesus defines this kind of unpardonable sin. (Having said that, let me correct it: Jesus does not use the term "unpardonable sin," and he does not even imply that the specific sin before us is unpardonable. Nevertheless, what he says leads to the identification of a specific sin with eternal doom. It is the one sin which, if unpardoned in life, will not be pardoned in death.)

What is this awful sin? Unbelief! Here is what Jesus says: "Whoever believes in (me) is not condemned, but whoever does not believe stands condemned already, because he has not believed in the name of God's one and only Son" (verse 18).

Judgment on sin was pronounced in the Garden of Eden. John Milton describes the scene in *Paradise Lost* (Book X, 205-208), where, grieving, God tells Adam that

> In the sweat of thy Face shalt thou eat Bread,
> Till thou return unto the ground, for thou
> Out of the ground was taken, know thy Birth,
> For dust thou art, and shalt to dust return.

More was involved than physical death. The judgment that follows death is far worse. Jesus spoke frequently of the dread possibility of eternal judgment. He divided men into two classes and said that he, as Son of Man, will someday say to those on his left, "Depart from me, you who are cursed, into the eternal fire prepared for the devil and his angels." The passage ends with Jesus' own description of the punishment awaiting the doomed. Said he, "They will go away to eternal punishment, but the righteous to eternal life" (Matthew 25:46).

In John 3 Jesus told Nicodemus (and, of course, he tells us also) that the judgment once pronounced upon a lost mankind rests upon those who do not believe in him. He who does not believe has been condemned already, and the judgment is not repealed in the case of those who do not believe in him.

What this means is that there is no sin so heinous as unbelief. Other sins may be vile; in God's sight *all* sins are vile, though some unquestionably viler than others. Murder is worse than the theft of a hubcap. Yet even murder may be forgiven. Before conversion, some of the members of the church in Corinth had been fornicators, adulterers, homosexuals, thieves, drunkards, swindlers, and perhaps a few other things. Yet they were forgiven (1 Corinthians 6:9-11).

There are plenty of fornicators, adulterers, homosexuals, thieves, etc. in Hell. Not one of those fornicators is in Hell because of his fornicating; not one of the thieves in Hell is there because of his crimes. The men and women in Hell, including respectable people as the world counts respectability, are there because they refused to believe in Jesus. Their sins—no matter how scarlet—could have been forgiven. Only one sin goes unforgiven—refusal to believe the gospel, refusal to believe in Jesus Christ.

God doesn't want anyone to be lost. He didn't send his Son to condemn the world, but so a condemned world could be saved (John 3:17). And all he asks is that he be taken seriously! He who believes in me, Jesus says, is not judged. He does not come into judgment; instead, he has passed out of death (i.e., the state of condemnation) into life.

Every soul in Hell knows why he or she is there—not because of specific sins, no matter how gross, but because of refusal to believe in Jesus. In life that sin went unpardoned, and in Hell it becomes unpardonable.

Think about it!

What does it mean to be lost?

The idea of lostness probably has its source in the Bible. When Jesus was friendly with a man named Zacchaeus, whom respectable people despised as a kind of polite outlaw, Jesus explained his action. "The Son of Man," he said, meaning himself, "has come to seek and to save what was lost" (Luke 19:10). Zacchaeus the sinner was "lost."

Another "lost" person was the prodigal son. He left his father's home and went to the far country where he lived it up until he was broke. Technically he wasn't really "lost"; he knew exactly where he was, and he knew the road home. But he was in great danger and eventually began to starve to death; and when he came to his senses he admitted it. "My father's hired men have food to spare," he moaned, "and here I am starving to death" (Luke 15:17). As some translations have it, he was "perishing."

Now that's interesting, because the Greek word sometimes translated "lost" is usually corrected to read "perishing" or "dying." When the disciples thought their frail boat was being swamped in the waves, they woke Jesus and shouted that they were perishing. And the Apostle Paul wrote that "if our gospel is veiled, it is veiled to those who are perishing" (2 Corinthians 4:3). There it is—that same word, sometimes translated "lost," but really meaning "to perish" or "to die."

The plain truth is that both ideas are true of non-Christians. They are "lost" in the sense of wandering far from God, and they are "perishing" in the sense that all lost souls are doomed. Physically, of course, everybody grows old and dies. But to perish or die in the biblical sense means to be forever banished from the presence of God, the world's true source of life. It means to be forever lost. Lost . . . forever lost! The words are like the tolling of a bell.

But nobody has to remain lost in this life. Jesus said he had come to seek and to save the lost. He seeks the lost, and he saves those who are perishing. It's reassuring to know that he came to the far country to search for us lost sinners. When he finds us, he brings us home to God—provided, of course, that we are willing to come. Jesus never comes on strong; he doesn't overwhelm people. He finds us, then gently invites us to come to him and find in him everything we need.

Why do human beings die?

Because we grow older every day, and weaker. Sooner or later vital parts cease to function, and we die. It would be dreadful to live forever in bodies that go on aging, having minds that lose their powers. The twelfth chapter of Ecclesiastes (verse 1) refers to old age as "the days of trouble . . . when you will say, 'I find no pleasure in them.' " For many, death comes as a blessed release from a crumbling prison house.

The question, of course, is why do we grow old. Death is only the final act in a series of physical collapses. Why must we grow old and die? Why has no one ever found the fabled elixir of life?

The answer is given in the Bible. "Just as sin entered the world through one man, and death through sin, and in this way death came to all men, because all sinned . . ." (Romans 5:12). There's the answer: death is the penalty for sin. It doesn't just happen; God demands it. Sickness and death are by no means purely genetic, though it is possible medical investigators may someday discover how death is transmitted genetically. What matters is that death (and its necessary preliminaries, sickness and aging) are judicial penalties handed down because of sin.

The testimony of Scripture, which is confirmed by the evidence visible on all sides, is that the entire creation was affected by sin. The cosmos itself bears the marks of Adam's disobedience. Every living creature must die sooner or later; vegetation decays, and even inanimate things like rocks age and crumble. The language of science usually refers to this sort of thing as "the law of entropy," or "the second law of thermodynamics." Whatever it is called, the important thing is to know that death and decay in the universe, as well as in human beings, came into the world through sin.

But there's no need for gloom, for Jesus conquered sin and the grave. The Apostle Paul wrote that "Christ Jesus . . . destroyed death and has brought life and immortality to light through the gospel" (2 Timothy 1:10). He was echoing the very words of Jesus, who promised his friends eternal life. "I tell you the truth," he said, "whoever hears my word and believes him who sent me has eternal life and will not be condemned; he has crossed over from death to life" (John 5:24).

The great hope of Christians—i.e., those who have surrendered themselves by faith to Jesus Christ—is victory over death. This may be realized by resurrection from the dead, or by instant transformation at Christ's coming. There are mysteries in life and in death, but this much is clear, that "death (will be) swallowed up in victory" (1 Corinthians 15:54). For those who love Jesus Christ our Lord, death is a broken foe, a temporary inconvenience.

What will happen to me when I die?

Hamlet, the prince of Denmark, was troubled in mind—whether to endure "the slings and arrows of outrageous fortune, / Or to take arms against a sea of troubles, / And by opposing end them? To die: to sleep; / No more; and by a sleep to say we end / The heartache and natural shocks / That flesh is heir to, 'tis a consummation / Devoutly to be wished. . . ." The trouble was, he didn't know what happens after death. It would be easy to end his misery with a bare bodkin, but would he dream in death? "To sleep; perchance to dream: ay, there's the rub; / For in that sleep of death what dreams may come, / When we have shuffled off this mortal coil, / Must give us pause" (III.i.56).

In the ancient world death was regarded with horror and hopelessness. The horror is understandable in view of man's powerful instinct for living and his inability to explain death. What is death? More to the point, what happens to the real me when I die? None of the ancient world's philosophers could answer these questions.

A sense of hopelessness is also understandable. After all, who has ever returned from the grave? Those who die are gone, gone forever; and nothing can bring them back. In Thessalonica, an ancient town in what is now known as Turkey, a monument was found with these words inscribed on it: "after death no returning; from the grave, no rising." Could any words more powerfully express the hopelessness of death?

Many centuries have passed since those words were chiseled on stone, but the sentiment expressed still prevails. Most people think of death as quite horrible and hopeless—if they think about it at all. Christians are willing to think about it and talk about it, and Christians who know their Bibles feel no need to use euphemistic terms such as "passed away" for "died." When *they* resort to such terms, the idea is not to conceal the truth about death, but to reveal its deepest meaning for those for whom death no longer holds any real terrors.

What *does* happen to people who die?

Death is the separation of the immaterial part of man (soul/spirit) from the material (the body). Once this happens, the body begins immediately to decompose. In biblical language, dust returns to dust. Everybody knows this, including Hamlet, and even in our society where corpses are embalmed and decorated, there is no concealing the essential starkness of death. The most benumbed mourner knows that the body will return to the elements. The question, then, concerns the fate of the immaterial part, the soul. What happens to it?

The answer is, it—i.e., he or she—goes to Heaven or Hell. For the soul of the departed there is no third alternative. This is made quite clear in a statement of our Lord which was recorded by Matthew (25:46). Speaking of certain persons, he said, "They will go away to eternal punishment, but the righteous to eternal life." He also said that at the end of the age the angels would sever the wicked from among the righteous and cast them into the furnace of fire (Matthew 13:49, 50). In fact, he had more to say about Hell than anyone else.

But he also held out the hope of eternal life. There are more references than can be cited here, but perhaps an example or two will serve to illustrate the sort of thing he promised. Here's what he said: "My sheep listen to my voice; I know them, and they follow me. I give them eternal life and they shall never perish; no one can snatch them out of my hand" (John 10:27, 28). If that doesn't excite us, nothing will. However, here's another example of the sort of thing Jesus said about eternal life: "For my Father's will is that everyone who looks to the Son and believes in him shall have eternal life, and I will raise him up at the last day" (John 6:40).

What did he mean? The apostles understood him to mean an immediate grant of eternal life, and the hope of physical resurrection in God's own time. So what happens when a believer dies? He goes to Heaven. The Apostle Paul said, "We . . . know that as long as we are at home in the body we are away from the Lord. We live by faith, not by sight. We are confident, I say, and would prefer to be away from the body and at home with the Lord" (2 Corinthians 5:6-8). For a Christian, then, death means to be "at home with the Lord."

The Apostle Paul said as much about death as perhaps any of the apostles. He spoke of his own approaching death as a "departure" (2 Timothy 4:6). He meant that the real Paul, the inner man, would at death depart from his body and from the earth itself. But for Paul the term departure embraced two concepts: a leaving and an arriving. Everybody knows what is meant by the leaving, but only those who know and believe their Bibles know what is meant by arriving.

Paul explains the concept in more than one place. For example, he writes from prison that he has a desire "to depart (the leaving) and be with Christ" (the arriving) (Philippians 1:23). The two concepts were virtually one in Paul's mind. To depart is to be with Christ. To leave is to arrive, and one arrives at the place where Christ is. That this is precisely what Paul means is clear from a passage we have already examined where, speaking of death, he explains that death is an absence (absent from the body) and a presence (present with the Lord) (2 Corinthians 5:8).

Consequently, Paul was always courageous in the face of difficulties. Even when his life was threatened he knew that there are worse things than death. He would make a journey, so to speak. He would be absent from his body but immediately present with the Lord. Thus, he would both leave and arrive.

For those who know the Lord Jesus, this is a comforting hope, isn't it?

Any medical man can tell you what happens *at* death: the heart stops beating, and the brain ceases to register anything on an electro-encephalogram. But what happens next?

Many believe that nothing happens. Death, they say, is the end of the road. It doesn't take much reflection to realize that those who make such assertions can't prove the truth of their statements. Maybe they just like to think that death is the end. This much is certain: nobody has ever returned from death specifically to tell us about it. So there are no experts in the field; an illiterate witchdoctor knows as much about what comes after death as does the most learned academic.

The only reliable source of information we have is the Bible. The Bible is revealed truth. *Revealed* means that nobody discovered it for himself; God revealed the peculiar truths contained in the Bible. One of these concerns death and afterwards, and the substance of it is that man survives the destruction of his body. In speaking of his own death Job said, "After my skin has been destroyed, yet in my flesh shall I see God" (Job 19:26). He was one of the first to affirm the great truth of survival after death.

The Bible teaches that man does not merely survive—he faces God. In one place it is written that "man is destined to die once, and after that to face judgment" (Hebrews 9:27). It appears from other passages that judgment does not follow immediately upon death. Our Lord spoke of a coming time when all who are in the tombs will come forth, some to a resurrection of life and others to a resurrection of judgment.

Thus, judgment may not immediately follow death. However, those who die do not exist in a kind of limbo waiting for judgment-day. Our Lord once pulled a curtain aside and showed that those who die are immediately comforted or tormented, as the case may be.

The determining factor is one's response in life to the Word of God. Those who hear it—i.e., hear in the sense of accepting it, which means accepting the Lord of whom it speaks—are saved. Those who reject it—i.e., reject him—are lost. When they die, they cannot join the Christ whom they rejected in life. They go to Hell; there is no other place for them.

It was uncertainty about what comes after death that kept Hamlet from killing himself. He termed death "that undiscover'd country from whose bourn / No traveller returns," and dread of what we might find there makes us willing to "rather bear those ills we have / Than fly to others that we know not of." Yet the plain teaching of the Bible is that one need not dread what comes after death. It is possible to know with assurance that you are going to Heaven. Uncertainty about so important a matter derives either from ignorance of what God says about it, or an unwillingness to believe it.

Peter wrote plainly: "Praise be to the God and Father of our Lord Jesus Christ! In his great mercy he has given us new birth into a living hope through the resurrection of Jesus Christ from the dead, and into an inheritance that can never perish, spoil or fade—kept in heaven for you, who through faith are shielded by God's power until the coming of the salvation that is ready to be revealed in the last time" (1 Peter 1:3-5).

The Apostle Paul wrote in Romans 8, ". . . neither death nor life, neither angels nor demons, neither the present nor the future, nor any powers, neither height nor depth, nor anything else in all creation, will be able to separate us from the love of God that is in Christ Jesus our Lord."

The apostles obviously believed that possession of eternal life included immediate entrance into Heaven when they died. Paul spoke for all of them when he said that for him, to live was Christ and to die was gain. How could death be gain if it didn't open a door into Heaven? That he believed he would go immediately to Heaven is even clearer in his next statement: "I desire to depart and be with Christ, which is better by far" (Philippians 1:21-24).

Anyone can have that same assurance. All it takes is faith that Jesus is the Christ, and that he will forgive your sins if you entrust your soul to him. "To all who received him . . . he gave the right to become children of God" (John 1:12). Salvation is a kind of package deal. It includes not only forgiveness, fellowship with God even now, membership in a worldwide brotherhood, but also the assurance of an eternal home which you will possess when you die.

Is Hell real?

In a book published in 1944, the French philosopher-novelist Jean Paul Sartre gave his definition of Hell. "Hell is—other people!" That remark says more about Jean Paul Sartre that it does about Hell. T. S. Eliot's definition of Hell is only slightly better. In "The Cocktail Party," he says: ". . . Hell is oneself, / Hell is alone, the other figures in it / Merely projections." Neither definition is worth much; they manifest a mood rather than information derived from an authoritative source. The fact is, they echo Marlowe's *Dr. Faustus.*

And yet, there may be an element of truth hiding in each statement. Is Hell other people? Not now, to be sure. In his autobiography the philosopher-atheist Bertrand Russell says that the presence of one's friends is all that makes life tolerable. What else is there in life, he asks? But to be confined forever with the kinds of people God excludes from his eternal home—surely that would turn a garden into a Hell.

Or to dwell alone with never the sound of an echoing voice! Alone with a mind awake to relive sins long forgotten, to be alone with thoughts of lost opportunities—to see them all as if on a reel that goes round and round and never stops! Surely that would be dreadful! Was T. S. Eliot right when he said "Hell is oneself,/Hell is alone"? Or was Sartre right? Is Hell other people?

Not quite, for Hell is more than a state of mind. It is a place, though certainly not the kind of place Shelley had in mind when he wrote that "Hell is a city much like London— / A populous and smoky city." The smokiest city in the world is a garden of delights by comparison with the real Hell, the place described in the Bible.

It would take a detailed study of the actual words of the Bible to formulate what may be termed the "doctrine of hell," that is, a biblical definition of it. But it is immediately evident that Hell is a place of torment. Terms such as "unquenchable fire," "furnace of fire," "torment in fire and brimstone," "the lake that burns with fire and brimstone," "the place prepared for the devil and his angels," and "the blackness of darkness" are unmistakable in their intent. The Scriptures require belief in a *place* of punishment. And to those who protest that the language of Scripture should not be taken literally, that there cannot be a real "lake" of fire and brimstone, it can be said that the reality cannot fail to surpass in horror the vision created by word-pictures.

What really matters is that we turn from our evil ways and flee in faith to the Savior. God has no pleasure in the ruin of sinners. Hell was made for the Devil and his angels, not for people. In Charles Wesley's words:

> Sinners, turn, why will ye die?
> God, your Maker, asks you why . . .
> Spiritually dead in sin,
> Dead, already dead within,
> Spiritually dead in sin,
> Dead to God while here you breathe,
> Pant ye after second death?
> Will you still in sin remain,
> Greedy of eternal pain?
> O ye dying sinners, why,
> Why will you forever die?

What will Hell be like?

Job was contemptuous of criminal types, especially murderers, seducers, and thieves. "Such men are scum on the surface of the water," he said. But they won't last long; as drought and summer heat make away with snow, so does Sheol make away with the sinner.

And once dead, he is quickly forgotten. "Even a mother will forget him," Job said, and "the worm feeds sweetly til he is remembered no more" (Job 24:18, NEB).

This is a gruesome vision of death. In life, the criminal struts and brags; once dead, he is only a feasting place for maggots. The maggots feed sweetly "til he is remembered no more." And, of course, the maggots themselves die, having no more corpse to sustain them.

Was Jesus thinking of that passage in Job when he spoke of a place where the worm does not die? In Hell, he said, "their worm does not die, and the fire is not quenched" (Mark 9:48). What does he mean by worms that don't die?

This strange-sounding phrase occurs in a passage in which Jesus taught that even a small act of service done to another would be rewarded, whereas a disservice (i.e., a seduction to sin) would be punished. "Anyone who gives you a cup of water in my name because you belong to Christ will certainly not lose his reward" (verse 41). On the other hand, to induce young believers to sin is so outrageous an act that it would be better to die first, and thus avoid disaster. There are worse things than early death. Dying is better than corrupting someone else. "It would be better for him to be thrown into the sea with a millstone tied around his neck than for him to cause one of these little ones to sin" (Luke 17:2). That's powerful language, but it expresses God's attitude toward those who cause others to sin.

It is also wrong to permit yourself to sin. Actually, the word *sin* is not used here; the word in question is "to stumble," or "cause to stumble." He who stumbles fails to enter into life (Mark 9:43) or the Kingdom of God (verse 47). Instead, he is thrown into Hell, "where their worm does not die, and the fire is not quenched." The word "hell" is a translation of the Greek *geena*, which is in turn a transliteration of the Hebrew *ge hinnom*, meaning "the valley of Hinnom." It usually appears in the Bible as Gehenna.

In the early days of Israel's history the people offered their children to the pagan god Molech (2 Kings 23:10; Jeremiah 7:31; 19:2-6). Good King Josiah stopped that, and the valley became Jerusalem's city dump. Fires burned more or less continually, reducing the garbage to ashes and at the same time keeping the maggot population to a minimum. When rain fell the fires smoldered or were quenched, and maggots multiplied. It takes little imagination to picture the place—a foul trench filled with reeking garbage, offal, and wriggling maggots.

In time Gehenna became for the Jews a symbol of the place of eternal torment. It was their word for what we mean when we say Hell. In Hell, however, the worm does not die and the fire is not quenched; the misery is permanent, without relief. Gehenna is the same as the lake of fire (Revelation 19:20; 20:10, 14).

It isn't necessary to think of Hell in terms of literal worms. The worm may represent unending remorse and the consciousness of unforgiven sins. The fire represents the action of divine wrath. To those who are lost, God is "a consuming fire" (Hebrews 12:29). Mark 9:49 says that everyone (of those who are lost) shall be "salted with fire." Apparently salt and fire are alike. Since salt is a preservative, the meaning may be that the fire of Hell does not destroy; it preserves. So it may be considered a kind of spiritual fire, acting on the consciousness of the lost.

Whatever the imagery intended, the prospect of eternal torment in Hell is too horrible to contemplate. And yet that is precisely what we must contemplate.

When Jesus saw the crowds, he had compassion on them, because they were harassed and helpless, like sheep without a shepherd. . . . "I am the good shepherd." (Matthew 9:36; John 10:11)

And my God will meet all your needs according to his glorious riches in Christ Jesus. (Philippians 4:19)

God made him who had no sin to be sin for us, so that in him we might become the righteousness of God. (2 Corinthians 5:21)

Christ died for sins once for all, the righteous for the unrighteous, to bring you to God. (1 Peter 3:18)

3/WHAT HAS GOD DONE TO MEET MY NEEDS?

We all have specific needs in our lives. And we all want to know specifically what God has done to make our lives complete. How has his love taken action on our behalf?

Can a person really know before he dies that he will go to Heaven?

Anyone can know with assurance where he will spend eternity. This is one of the clearest messages in the Bible. Uncertainty about so important a matter derives from failure to know what God says, or an unwillingness to believe it.

A very clear statement about this question was made by Peter. Here's what he said: "Praise be to the God and Father of our Lord Jesus Christ! In his great mercy he has given us new birth into a living hope through the resurrection of Jesus Christ from the dead, and into an inheritance that can never perish, spoil or fade—kept in heaven for you, who through faith are shielded by God's power until the coming of the salvation that is ready to be revealed in the last time" (1 Peter 1:3-5).

One of my favorite passages is found in Romans 8. The Apostle Paul wrote, ". . . neither death nor life, neither angels nor demons, neither the present nor the future, nor any powers, neither height nor depth, nor anything else in all creation, will be able to separate us from the love of God that is in Christ Jesus our Lord" (verses 38, 39).

The Apostle John explained the purpose of his writings in his first letter when he said that he had written "to you who believe in the name of the Son of God so that you may *know* that you have eternal life" (5:13).

How can I find God?

The Book of Job may be the oldest book in the world, and it is certainly one of the most fascinating. The book is about Job, a suffering man who came to believe that God had turned away from him. His friends were poor comforters; they told him he was a secret sinner whom God was punishing. In desperation Job cried out, "If only I knew where to find him; if only I could go to his dwelling" (Job 23:3). But there was no way Job could find God at that time, since all he wanted was a chance to harangue God and justify himself before God. One of his friends said, "Touching the Almighty, we cannot find him out. . . . He respecteth not any that are wise of heart" (Job 37:23, 24, KJV).

Was Job's friend right? Partly. God does not regard those who are wise in their own conceits—i.e., those who think they have no need of him—but he can be found. In fact, that's what the Bible is all about. Psalm 34 says that "those who seek the Lord lack no good thing" (verse 10). The Psalms are full of promises to those who seek the Lord, and Isaiah 55 says: "Seek the Lord while he may be found; call on him while he is near. Let the wicked forsake his way and the evil man his thoughts. Let him turn to the Lord, and he will have mercy on him, and to our God, for he will freely pardon."

But Job's question still troubles many. Where can a person find God?

The first thing to settle in your mind is the fact that God does exist. The Bible does not attempt to prove this; it assumes the existence of God. "In the beginning God created the heavens and the earth" (Genesis 1:1)—that's the way the Bible begins. Much later, it says that "without faith it is impossible to please God, because anyone who comes to him must believe that he exists and that he rewards those who earnestly seek him" (Hebrews 11:6). So the first step in finding God is believing that he exists and that finding him is worth the effort.

Believing that he exists is easy. Paul suggested that in all of us there is a kind of innate perception of God (Romans 1:19, 20; Acts 17:28). This is an inborn capacity for believing in God when the idea is presented to us. Nobody needs a Bible to tell him God is; races or tribes that never heard of the Bible have a consciousness of God. Whether the idea is intuitive or the result of reason doesn't really matter; what matters is that belief in God is universal.

Finding him—that's the problem. In ancient Athens it was a problem too. They had an altar dedicated to "the unknown god" (Acts 17). When the Apostle Paul saw that altar, he felt sick at heart because of the people's ignorance of God. So he told them about God—not, to be sure, discoveries he had made through independent research, but truth which God had revealed. That's the crucial point—that while we may have an instinctive idea of God, we know nothing about him (his character, his acts—in short, his Being) unless he reveals the information. That's what Paul passed on to the pagans in Athens—knowledge about God which God himself had revealed.

The gist of Paul's talk is that God speaks to men through his Son, Jesus Christ. Others pointed out the same truth. The Apostle John admitted that no man had seen God at any time. But, he said, "the only begotten God, who is in the bosom of the Father, he has explained him" (John 1:18, NASB). One translation of the same verse puts it this way: "God's only Son, he who is nearest to the Father's heart, he has made him known" (NEB).

So, there's your answer. If you know Jesus Christ, you know God. One of the friends of Jesus got the message straight from the lips of Jesus. It was Philip who said to him, "Lord, show us the Father." Show us God—that's what he meant. Jesus made it plain. "Anyone who has seen me has seen the Father" (John 14:9). There couldn't be a simpler answer than that. If we have found Jesus Christ—whom we find through faith, believing his words as we read them in the Bible—we have found God.

Since there are so many religions in the world, how can Christians say there is only one way to God?

One reason is that some religions don't even try to show the way to God. Take animism, the religion of primitive peoples all over the world. That religion may be defined as a system of ceremonies designed to placate hostile spirit beings. If they even have a concept of God, it is vague and ill-defined. Their religion says nothing about finding him—whoever he may be.

The same is true of any polytheistic religion. As for oriental religions, release from the tyranny of seemingly endless reincarnations is the goal, not a personal relationship with the living God. Or in their view, God may include everything in the universe—even the flutter of a leaf. Their concept of God is utterly different from the God of the Bible. So it's necessary to discover what a religion claims to do for its adherents, and the nature of the god envisaged by the worshipers.

Christianity is unique, and its claims are unique. Unlike most religions in the world, Christianity claims to be a revelation from the living God. Further, it is based on the claims of a Man who lived in time and was reported to have done certain miracles, been crucified, and raised from the dead by the power of God. His existence can be verified historically, and what he said about himself can be verified. In fact, no events in ancient history have better historical documentation than the events associated with Jesus of Nazareth.

What kind of claims did he make for himself? Well, he said he could forgive sins. He also said that if anyone did not honor him, they were not honoring God the Father (see Mark 2:5; John 5:23ff.). He claimed to be the way, the truth, and the life, and said that no one could possibly come to God except through him (John 14:6-14). Those were truly astonishing claims! But he made an even greater one—he said that anyone who had seen him had seen God the Father.

It should be obvious that claims of that sort demand a reply. Either he was what he said he was or he was insane. A third possibility, I suppose, is that he was a deceiver—a kind of con man. But not even his worst enemies really believe that the Jesus of history was either a charlatan or insane. That leaves only one conclusion—that he was who he said he was—the Son of God (i.e., truly

God). If so, the claim that Christianity is the only way to God makes sense; in fact, the logic of it is irresistible. All that amazes Christians is that anyone should refuse to come to Christ for what he alone can offer—forgiveness of sins and eternal life.

Jesus said, "He who is not with me is against me." Must I take sides?

Choosing to follow Jesus Christ places me on his side—along with every other true believer in him. The alternative is—for me—unthinkable, since hostility to Jesus puts one in Satan's corner. Surely it is significant that the statement already quoted—i.e., "He who is not with me is against me"—was made in reply to certain persons who saw Jesus casting out demons and said he did it with Satan's help (Matthew 12:22-30). It was quite stupid of them because, as Jesus explained, why should Satan be expected to destroy his own kingdom?

The idea behind the explanation is that nobody can be both for and against some*thing* or some*one* at the same time. You're either for or against. By casting out demons Jesus showed plainly that he was against Satan, which made the accusation that he was doing it with Satan's help superstupid—and wicked.

This accusation was wicked because it revealed a deep-seated antagonism to Jesus in his accusers' hearts. This is why he said, "He who is not with me is against me." It was impossible for him to be both for and against Satan; it was equally impossible for the accusers of Jesus to be for and against him. Their attitude and their words showed plainly where they stood: they were against him.

And their stand brought terrible consequences. Jesus said, "Whoever believes in the Son has eternal life, but whoever rejects the Son will not see life, for God's wrath remains on him" (John 3:36).

Later the Apostle Paul said virtually the same thing; he warned his readers that the day was coming when the Lord Jesus would be revealed from Heaven with his mighty angels in flaming fire, dealing out retribution to those who do not know God, and to those who "do not obey the gospel of our Lord Jesus." These, he said, "will be punished with everlasting destruction and shut out from the presence of the Lord and from the majesty of his power" (2 Thessalonians 1:7ff.).

Every one of those words is weighty and solemn. They hint (for that's the best language can do when speaking of eternal damnation) at what it will cost Christ's enemies to be against him.

As for me, I'm on his side—which really means that he is for me. And "if God is for us, who can be against us?" (Romans 8:31).

What does it mean to be justified by faith?

If Romans 3:23 ended in a period, we'd all be sunk. Here's what the verse says: "For all have sinned and fall short of the glory of God. . . ." That's not the end of the statement—not by a long shot. But what follows is given a new verse number, and a reader could easily overlook the comma at the end of verse 23 and miss the essential connection with what follows. The sentence does not end with the flat statement that everybody falls short of the glory of God; it has much more to give than a doomsday pronouncement.

The actual wording varies from translation to translation, but the connection is unmistakable. The comma after the words about falling short of the glory of God is most important; it tells us to pause and get set for a tremendous message. What message? That sinners may be justified freely by God's grace! Even that is not the end of the sentence; it also gives the basis for free salvation, which, roughly, is what is meant by justification. Here's the complete thought: "For all have sinned and fall short of the glory of God, and are justified freely by his grace through the redemption that is in Christ Jesus." *Now* it's okay to punctuate with a period or a semicolon; the thought is complete.

Instead of telling us that we are doomed, God tells us that rescue is at hand. True, we sinned and we fail to make the grade spiritually. Nevertheless, God is willing to accept us freely. Accept us—that's what is meant by God's offer of justification. As used in the Bible, the word *justified* has richer meanings than when used in, say, a debate or a courtroom. A justified man—in biblical terms—is never vindicated, as is so often its meaning in secular terms. For example, killers are sometimes acquitted and released on the grounds that they had committed justifiable homicide. The killer was said to have been justified in what he did. Provocation was so extreme, he was justified in shooting his enemy. So in court he was vindicated. Justified, vindicated—the words carry virtually the same denotation in a case such as was just described.

In God's courtroom no one beats the rap on such a plea; no one is ever justifiably guilty of any sin, no one is ever vindicated. The verse says flatly, "for all have sinned and fall short of the glory of God. . . ." "Fall short," not vindicated. Nevertheless, those who "fall short" may be "justified." What does it mean if it doesn't mean vindicated? In simple terms it means accepted. We sinners fall short of God's glory. Yet he accepts us freely. He welcomes us. Instead of slamming the door on us and throwing away the key, he opens it wide to those who have sinned and forfeited any expectation of an invitation; then he says, Come in. The basis for it? "The redemption that came by Christ Jesus," our "sacrifice of atonement" (verses 24, 25).

Why should I believe in Jesus Christ?

The Gospel according to John is believed by many to be the most profound document in the New Testament. Yet John conveys truth in simple language. He uses short, familiar words such as life, light, and love. One of his favorite words is the verb "to believe." Curiously, he does not use the noun form, "belief," but only the verb, "to believe."

John uses this verb ninety-nine times in his Gospel. In his first epistle he defines it. "We accept man's testimony, but God's testimony is greater because it is the testimony of God, which he has given about his Son" (1 John 5:9). So believing is receiving as true the testimony that someone gives. It means to be persuaded of the truth of something. John says that we receive the testimony men give. Under normal circumstances we believe each other. If the dentist tells me he will fix my teeth on Monday at 5 P.M., I go to his office on Monday at 5 P.M. And if I request telephone service, the telephone company installs the telephone, believing that I will pay the bill.

This is somewhat remarkable because our word is not always reliable. Why not? At least three reasons for caution may be cited. First, I can lie. I can also misinterpret what I heard or saw, so that my version of a conversation or an event is distorted. I do not intentionally lie, but what I say is not true. Finally, I can forget the truth about something, and in attempting to recall it confuse fancy with fact.

Nevertheless, we believe each other. Society could not function if we did not take at face value what people tell us. If I don't believe the dentist when he tells me to come on Monday at 5 P.M., how do I get my teeth fixed—camp on his doorway until he lets me in?

John's point is that it should be infinitely easier to believe God than to believe each other. Why? Because God does not lie, does not misunderstand what he hears or sees, and does not forget. Accordingly, his testimony is 100 percent true. Because God's word is truth, refusal to receive it as true is the same as calling him a liar (1 John 5:10). If you don't believe *me*, you don't necessarily call me a liar. You say that I am mistaken, that I have forgotten what really happened, or that I am just plain confused—which may be the case. But God makes no mistakes, remembers everything, and is never confused. Hence, if his word is not true, it is a lie. But who is really prepared to call God a liar?

Not many people are quite so foolhardy. Nevertheless, many in effect call him a liar. How? By refusing to receive his word as recorded in the Bible. Jesus condemned men living in his time who did not believe him (John 8:21, 24). "Whoever does not believe stands condemned already" Jesus said (John 3:18). This means that all who have not believed the gospel are in a state of condemnation, even while they are living. They live in "the domain of darkness," waiting for death—which will place them forever beyond hope of salvation (Colossians 1:13).

Let's end on a positive note. After all, the gospel is 100 percent positive. Jesus says, "He who believes in (me) is not condemned." Have you accepted this alternative? Have you received God's word as true and put your faith and hope in Christ Jesus? If so, you are no longer under a cloud; you are not judged, not condemned. And it isn't I who say this; it is the testimony of God himself.

What does it mean to "repent"?

Not long after John the Baptist began to preach, he was arrested and thrown into a dungeon. He had not broken any laws, but he had rebuked a local king for having married his own brother's wife. John told him this was wrong. The king knew it was wrong, and he admitted that John was a righteous and holy man. The woman in the case, however, admitted nothing. The Bible says she "nursed a grudge against John and wanted to kill him" (Mark 6:19). Knowing she was capable of it, Herod, the king, put John under protective custody.

It didn't work. The woman tricked the king into consenting to the execution of John. This happened at a party where everybody got drunk and called for girls to dance for them. The king was so pleased with his step-daughter's performance that he promised her whatever she requested. Coached by her mother, she asked for John's head on a platter, and the king stupidly gave orders for the execution.

This cost him his soul, as subsequent events proved, and it sickened Jesus. John was his friend. With John's death, it was obvious to Jesus that the time had come for him to begin a public ministry. So, the Bible says, Jesus began to preach "the good news of God" (Mark 1:14). "The kingdom of God is near," he said, "Repent and believe the good news!" As his advance man had called listeners to repentance, so Jesus also emphasized repentance. "Repent and believe the good news." A legitimate inference is that belief in the good news is impossible without repentance. If so, what is repentance?

The answer is, repentance means to turn. Every Jew familiar with his Hebrew Bible should have known that. God told the prophet Ezekiel to say to the people of Israel, "As I live, declares the Sovereign Lord, I take no pleasure in the death of the wicked, but rather that they turn from their ways and live. Turn! Turn from your evil ways! Why will you die, O house of Israel?" (Ezekiel 33:11ff.). Another prophet, Hosea, urged his listeners to return to the Lord God. "Return, O Israel, to the Lord your God. Your sins have been your downfall! Take words with you and return to the Lord. Say to him: 'Forgive all our sins and receive us graciously, that we may offer the fruit of our lips' " (Hosea 14:12).

So Jesus' listeners should have understood his call to repentance. He was by no means the first to insist upon it, but he was the most authoritative. God spoke *through* the prophets (Hebrews 1:1), but he spoke *in* his Son. Jesus was no mere channel for messages from God; his voice was the voice of God himself. Thus, it was authoritative, and none could disregard it safely. As he himself said to his own generation, "The men of Nineveh will stand up at the judgment with this generation and condemn it; for they repented at the preaching of Jonah, and now one greater than Jonah is here" (Matthew 12:41).

The men of Nineveh are going to be busy at the judgment; they'll be witnesses against every generation since the days of Christ, including our own. God is speaking to us in his Son, and if we don't listen and turn from our sins, what a pity! Rather, what a calamity!

Have any real miracles ever occurred?

What is a miracle? Not until we know what miracles are can we say whether or not they have occurred.

Webster's Seventh (New Collegiate Dictionary) defines a miracle as an extraordinary event manifesting a supernatural work of God, or an extremely outstanding or unusual event, thing, or accomplishment.

Nobody can deny that miracles have occurred if we use the second definition, since unusual things do happen from time to time. According to this definition, unexpected cures are sometimes termed "miracles," and why not—if a miracle is nothing more than an unusual event, thing, or accomplishment.

However, the question asked here presupposes the first, more difficult definition: a miracle is an extraordinary event manifesting a supernatural work of God. Now we have to decide whether this kind of miracle *can* happen. If such miracles can't happen, they obviously have not happened.

Many people refuse to believe in the possibility of such miracles. They say there is no God, nature is all there is, and they reason—logically—that miracles can't happen. There is no way an unbeliever can be convinced that miracles as defined here have actually happened since, according to his system, they *can't* happen. If nature is all there is, how can something supernatural take place?

But if you accept the existence of God and believe that God created the world of nature, then it isn't difficult to believe in the possibility of miracles. God is able to do what he wants to do in his world; he can act supernaturally—that is, he can introduce into the operation of what we call nature something unexpected. If God exists, why should it be considered incredible that miracles can occur?

That, incidentally, is the question the Apostle Paul asked a prominent man in the first century. "Why does it seem incredible to you all that God should raise the dead?" (Acts 26:8, *Phillips*). That brings us to the question of whether the miracles which can happen have actually happened. The answer, quite simply, is yes. Paul admits that he himself was reluctant to believe what he had heard about Jesus. But eventually he was persuaded to do so; the evidence in support of the miracle of Christ's birth, the miracles which he did in his lifetime, and the miracle of his resurrection was simply overwhelming.

If you think about it, you have to agree with Paul that it is not incredible that God can raise the dead. And if you take time to study, you'll have to agree also that God did in fact raise Jesus from the dead. As Paul says, the thing "was not done in a corner."

Do miracles still happen today?

In one of Shakespeare's comedies an old lord makes an entrance marveling at the sudden improvement in the king's health. "They say miracles are past," he says in obvious bafflement. What does the Bible say?

As far as I know there is no specific verse that says miracles can't still happen. But not many important truths can be handled by appeal to a single text of Scripture. As for miracles, Scripture teaches that there were healers and workers of miracles in the early church. The ability to do such things was given to certain people by the Holy Spirit, according to 1 Corinthians 12:4-11. In that paragraph is a tabulation of the various gifts—i.e., endowments of the Holy Spirit, which he gives to Christians. Nobody is ignored; in fact, the language is quite emphatic about this. "To each," it says, "the manifestation of the Spirit is given for the common good" (verse 7).

However, there is no guarantee that the Holy Spirit gives the same gifts in every age. He gives a variety of gifts, to be sure, but not all to the same person, and perhaps not all in the same period of church history. To the early church he gave apostles—i.e., witnesses of the resurrection. But no subsequent church period has ever seen a genuine apostle. The same may be true of prophets now that we have the canon of Scripture.

As for healers and miracle-workers, they were needed in the early church to validate the message. More correctly, they validated the messengers; the message spoke for itself. Some ancient manuscripts include verses 9-20 in Mark 16, in which miracles are spoken of as signs. A more reliable passage is Hebrews 2:1-4, where it says that "God also testified to it (the message of salvation) by signs, wonders and various miracles, and gifts of the Holy Spirit distributed according to his will." With the growth of the church, the need for miracles declined. Eventually they ceased, except for periodic appearances of faith-healers and speakers in tongues. Whether these are manifestations of the gifts of the Holy Spirit or some other spirit must be determined by criteria other than a text of Scripture. Remembering that evil spirits have abilities considerably higher than humans, one should investigate carefully an alleged miracle in the light of general scriptural principles.

One thing is certain: if God is still giving men power to work miracles, he is also giving others spiritual insights that enable them to distinguish between the fake and the real. God abhors impostors, and he doesn't want his people to be gullible.

What did Jesus mean when he told Nicodemus "You must be born again"?

Nicodemus was perplexed by our Lord's solemn assertion that unless one is born again, he cannot see the kingdom of God (John 3). He should not have been perplexed; after all, the prophets—whose writings honored teachers like Nicodemus were supposed to know by heart—talked about the new birth. Had Nicodemus never read David's penitential Psalm in which he pleads with God to create in him a new heart (Psalm 51:10)?

The new birth is certainly emphasized in the New Testament. The expression "born again" or "born of God" is found six times in John's Gospel and six times in his first epistle. Peter also uses the term, and Paul talks about the concept in various ways. For example, he says that if anyone is "in Christ," he is "a new creation" (2 Corinthians 5:17) and that Christians are "made alive" by God (Ephesians 2:5).

Paul's terminology helps us understand what is meant by the terms "born again" or the "new birth." It is certainly *not* outward reformation, or mere conformity to a new code of some sort. Conformity is all the rabbis had to offer their converts—conformity to Judaism's requirements.

What then is the new birth? It is the change produced by the Holy Spirit of God. I did not say change of heart. The old heart—that is, the nature with which one comes into the world—is not changed; it remains the same. The *man* (or woman) is changed by the impartation of a new heart, a new life, which has its source in God, not in earthly parents. It isn't a genetic thing at all; it is a spiritual experience.

Certain passages make this clear. For example, Paul describes the experience as "the washing of rebirth and renewal by the Holy Spirit" (Titus 3:5). In another place Paul tells us to "put on the new self, created to be like God in true righteousness and holiness" (Ephesians 4:24). Peter described believers as "partakers of the divine nature" (2 Peter 1:4, KJV).

This, in few words, is what is meant by the term "born again." "Born-again" people are not renewed people; they are made new and different. They have something additional which others do not have—a new nature which only God can produce in them.

It is important to stress this biblical truth in these times. "Born again" and the "new birth" are debased terms bandied about by people who have no idea what they really mean. They think the words are descriptive of a denomination, or perhaps a religious subculture. Some people think it is cute to speak of such things as born-again appetites or a born-again football team.

This may be the "in" way to talk, but it can be very dangerous. Why? Because it may lull people into carelessness about the need to be born again in the way Jesus intended when he used the term. What he told Nicodemus is, in essence, that no matter how good you may be, you aren't good enough; and nothing you can do will make you good enough. You need a much more radical change than you can achieve by striving. You must be born again; you must be born from above. Otherwise, you are forever lost.

By the way, Nicodemus was not as dumb as some people make him out to be. When Jesus told him the truth that unless a man is born again he cannot see the kingdom of God, Nicodemus wanted to know how this could be done. He asked a question and half-answered it himself. The question was, "How can a man be born when he is old?" and his own answer of sorts was that he couldn't return to his mother's womb. Since everybody knows that, it doesn't appear to be a very bright remark.

But there was more to it than appears on the surface. He did not ask about birth in itself; he asked about birth with respect to an *old* person. What he meant was, can an old man like me be changed? Unlike his colleagues in the College of Pharisees, he was aware of inner inadequacies; he knew he was a sinner. If not, he'd never have come knocking at Jesus' door, nor would Jesus have given him so profound a discourse as he gave him that night. Nicodemus had no quarrel with Jesus' assertion about the need of a new birth, but he had difficulty believing it was possible for a man long set in his ways. In the light of human behavior, that was an understandable difficulty.

The real problem, of course, was that Nicodemus didn't know what the Lord was talking about. Jesus was thinking of a birth from God as contrasted with physical birth, which is simply human beings reproducing themselves. Nicodemus, on the other hand, couldn't think of a way to change other than to return to the womb for a kind of recycling—which he knew couldn't be done. His exclamation, "Surely (a man) cannot enter a second time into his mother's womb to be born!" is hauntingly sad. The words have the plaintive note of a man who wishes he could begin all over again, and knows he can't.

It wouldn't have done any good to begin all over again the way he began life the first time. "Flesh gives birth to flesh," Jesus said (John 3:6). What he meant was that Nicodemus needed something better than a second go-around; recycling the old man would make no basic changes. If he had any children, the evidence was there before him; in a sense, he was recycled every time he produced a son or daughter. In his children he saw himself—reborn, so to speak, yet not a whit different. His children were like him—human beings with every flaw common to the race. "Flesh gives birth to flesh." If he were reborn physically, he'd still be the same old Nicodemus— sighing about his sins.

Nobody can really change himself, not even by so drastic a measure as returning to the womb for a second crack at life. Everybody can take self-improvement courses, of course, and there's no excuse for anybody yielding habitually to his worst impulses. But the stuff of a human being is defective; the material from which we are made is flawed, and nothing can change it. Nothing short of a new life from God.

And that's exactly what God offers. Everyone who receives Jesus Christ into his life, believing in his name, receives new life from God.

How can I know I have been born again?

When Nicodemus raised his eyebrows after Jesus told him he (and everyone else in the world) needed to be born again, Jesus implied that the new birth is not something one gets by dint of effort. It is the work of the Holy Spirit of God. A born-again person is, in Jesus' words, "born of the Spirit." The Bible also says that born-again people are "born of God." Combined, the two statements teach that the new birth is a divine work. The Holy Spirit imparts new life to those who come to Christ in faith, so that they are "born of God."

How do you know you have been born again? The Holy Spirit is invisible, and there seems to be no way to watch him at work. To explain, Jesus drew an analogy between the wind and the Spirit. You can't see the wind, he said; yet you can hear it. Evidence of the wind's blowing is unmistakable; even a child can tell it. Similarly, evidence of the work of the Holy Spirit is unmistakable in those who are born of the Spirit.

What this means is that those who are born again know it. To outward appearances a regenerate person may be the same man. Though very different from what he was before conversion, his new manner of life may not impress onlookers favorably. They may not agree that the change is evidence of a spiritual birth. They may think that it is evidence of mental derangement or something similar.

Yet the man will know that he is different in a good sense. He may not understand what has happened; understanding comes with knowledge of what the Bible teaches. But he will know immediately that he is a new man or she is a new woman. And as he reads the Bible and prays, he will discover that the unseen source of inspiration for his new life is the Holy Spirit, who actually abides with him. He will learn that the Holy Spirit is the true source of the love, joy, peace, patience, kindness, goodness, faithfulness, gentleness, self-control and other Godlike qualities now present in his life.

This is what Jesus meant when he said, "So it is with everyone born of the Spirit." You heard the wind, he said. You will also "hear" the Holy Spirit in your life. The Unseen Presence will, like the wind, blow across your heart.

Whether Nicodemus grasped the significance of Jesus' words at the moment is not clear. Eventually, however, he did understand. He understood that Jesus was offering him a new possibility. Instead of exhortations to shape up or ship out, to reform himself or be damned, Nicodemus was offered new life. The Holy Spirit of God would do the work; all that was required of Nicodemus was willingness to come humbly, in faith receiving God's gift through Jesus Christ.

This is what God offers all of us—a new birth; and this is all he requires of *us*—faith to receive it humbly, at Jesus' feet.

Can I truly be forgiven for my sins?

Nobody reads Kipling anymore, but in his time he was fine. But his talk about "lesser breeds without the Law," and "the white man's burden" began to embarrass a generation living in the postcolonial era. Nowadays only children read Kipling—*The Jungle Books, The Just-So Stories,* and *Kim.* There may be other readers, older folks mainly, who pick up an old volume in an idle moment. They don't go unrewarded. Kipling has some magnificent lines, some of which have entered into the mainstream of our English language. For example, this: "The tumult and the shouting dies; / The captains and the Kings depart: / Still stands Thine ancient sacrifice, / An humble and a contrite heart."

But not everything Kipling wrote is memorable or true. Take this bitter line from "Tomlinson": "The sin ye do by two and two ye must pay for one by one." It is an arresting statement and it sends a chill into your bones. But is it true? Is divine justice so inexorable that sins must be paid for "one by one"? What does the Bible say?

The Apostle Paul says that "each of us will give an account of himself to God" (Romans 14:12). In another place he says, ". . . we must all appear before the judgment seat of Christ, that each one may receive what is due him for the things done in the body, whether good or bad" (2 Corinthians 5:10). At first glance, that seems to say that God keeps careful records and will make you pay for the evil you do in your life. Careful study reveals something entirely different. First, the two passages refer to Christians for whom, the same writer tells us elsewhere, there is no more judgment. Second, the issue is rewards, not punishment. Christ will evaluate our lives as Christians and reward us accordingly. There is no question of paying for specific sins. Those were all forgiven the moment we became Christians (cf. Romans 8:1).

Sins forgiven! There is no lovelier concept in Scripture than that! The Bible uses various terms to define salvation—terms such as redemption, reconciliation, regeneration, renewal, and others. But none is more comforting, more reassuring to a sinner's heart than forgiveness. As Paul says, "In him (i.e., in association with Jesus Christ through faith) we have redemption through his blood, the forgiveness of sins, in accordance with the riches of God's grace that he lavished on us" (Ephesians 1:7; cf. Colossians 1:14). Forgiven—

completely forgiven, according to the measure of the riches of God's grace. You can't find a more complete forgiveness than that.

The apostle labors the point. In his letter to Christians in Colosse he says that God "forgave us all our sins, having canceled the written code, with its regulations, that was against us . . ." Or, as one translation puts it, he "wiped out the damning evidence of broken laws and commandments which always hung over our heads . . ." (Colossians 2:14, *Phillips*). The verb translated "wiped out" is used in another place where God himself says he will not blot out of the book of life the names of his servants (Revelation 3:5). In another passage he says he will wipe away all tears. It's the same verb.

The apostles who used it may have taken it from the prophet Isaiah. Through the prophet God says, "I have swept away your offenses like a cloud" (Isaiah 44:22). When God forgives, he wipes the slate clean.

How about that, Mr. Kipling? Do you still believe that "the sin ye do two by two ye must pay for one by one"? Not for those who believe in Jesus Christ. For them, there is complete forgiveness. But you may be partly right, Mr. Kipling. Those who in this life reject Christ must appear before him to be judged "each person . . . according to what he had done" (Revelation 20:13).

Can I lose my salvation because of unconfessed sin?

Sometimes Christians die suddenly in auto wrecks or airplane crashes. They die with their sins unconfessed, or so their survivors think. Actually nobody knows what passes through the mind in that last brief moment before death. For all we know, a whole lifetime may zip through the mind faster than lightning, so that the doomed person may have had more than enough time to make his peace with God. Still, the question vexes us. Can we lose our salvation because of unconfessed sin?

The question assumes that we have salvation; otherwise, there would be nothing to lose. But this assumption raises still another question, how we received salvation in the first place. Was it given to us in return for a complete confession of all our sins, or was there some other basis for its bestowal? This is the crucial question, for salvation can be lost if it was granted conditionally.

The testimony of Scripture, however, is that salvation is given freely—i.e., without any strings attached. The candidate for salvation must meet certain requirements, to be sure. But these "requirements" are not the sort that demand performance on his part, or personal merit. Actually, there is only one requirement: faith in God. "Believe in the Lord Jesus, and you will be saved . . ." was Paul's reply to the jailer who begged in desperation for an answer to his question about the way to salvation. The same apostle reminded Christians in Ephesus that they had been saved "by grace . . . through faith" (Ephesians 2:8). The New Testament is full of similar statements, each demanding nothing more than faith in Christ.

Faith in Jesus Christ must be genuine, to be sure, and it is inevitably accompanied by, even preceded by, repentance. The Apostle Paul combined the ideas of repentance toward God and faith in our Lord Jesus Christ and said, in effect, "This is the proper, saving response to the gospel." This is what is required, this is what it takes *on your part* to become a Christian.

Nothing is said about confession, except that a penitent must confess Jesus as Lord. Check this in Romans 10:9. Unquestionably, a penitent will indeed confess his sins, or at least as many of them as crowd into his mind at the time. But the emphasis in Scripture is not on confession of sin; it is on believing God.

The point of all this is that since salvation is not given on the basis of confession of sin, it is not withdrawn because of unconfessed sins. By God's grace we are saved through faith, not confession of sins. If, then, salvation *could* be lost, it would be lost because of unbelief. But the plain teaching of Scripture is that salvation *cannot* be lost—not for any reason. It is not given conditionally in the first place. "The wages of sin is death," Paul explained, "but the gift of God is eternal life in Christ Jesus our Lord" (Romans 6:23).

Christians should remember, however, that while unconfessed sin will not cost them their souls, it will steal their joy and deprive them of fellowship with God and there will be loss. Paul warned his friends about that possibility (see 1 Corinthians 3:15). He was unwilling to be ashamed in the Lord's presence, and that fear alone was sufficient to make him keep short accounts with God. It should suffice for us also.

What can God do for me?

The Apostle Paul made a number of great statements about God, but none greater than one found in Romans 10 (verse 12): "the same Lord is Lord of all and richly blesses all who call on him." A theologian might like the concept of the unity of God that it presents: God is one, or there is one God—that sort of thing. A poor sinner, on the other hand, would unquestionably cling to the second thought—that God richly blesses all who call on him.

What does it mean? Different translations sometimes help. They express the Greek in slightly different ways, such as this: He is "abounding in riches for all who call on him." Or this: "He is rich enough for the need of all who invoke him." Or this: His "boundless resources are available to all who turn to him in faith." And a very old translation (Moule) reads that he is "wealthy to all who call to him." Together, these various renderings make the message plain: the inexhaustible resources of a wealthy God are made available to all who turn to him in faith.

But what kind of resources? What is the nature of the riches God lavishes on those who invoke him? Material things? Houses? Cars? Good jobs? No, not those things! Then what? The answer is found in Paul's own use of the term. In the Letter to the Romans he refers to God's riches five or six times. For example, there are "the riches of his kindness, tolerance and patience" (2:4), and "the riches of the wisdom and knowledge of God" (11:33). Paul also spoke of "the riches of God's grace" (Ephesians 1:7), which he described elsewhere as "incomparable riches" (Ephesians 2:7; cf. 1 Timothy 6:17; Hebrews 11:26). So the resources God places at our disposal are his own character in all its fullness and gifts in keeping with that character—such as forgiveness of sins. Paul wrote his friends in Ephesus that in Christ (i.e., as brought close to him in a living, personal relationship) we have "redemption through his blood, the forgiveness of sins, in accordance with the riches of God's grace that he lavished on us with all wisdom and understanding" (Ephesians 1:7, 8).

Now those are gifts worth having! But no ordinary giver could offer them. Who but God can offer forgiveness of sins? And who else's offer would mean anything? The only one whose forgiveness we want or need is the One who has power to cast us into Hell. But can God really forgive us? Can he forget the past, wipe out our sins as if they had never existed? Can he receive us as if we were genuinely clean and guiltless?

The answer is yes. But not without a price—to himself. Paul explained it. We have redemption, he said, through Christ's blood (Ephesians 1:7). There's the answer: Christ's blood. That bloody death which he died at Calvary made it possible for a holy God to lavish his treasures on unholy men and women. Christ's cross atones for sin; it opens God's storehouse of treasures and invites us inside. Come to me, he says, and I will give you whatever your soul requires.

How can one find peace of mind?

More than 200 years have passed since the French philosopher Pascal recorded his little analysis of the state of man. He used three words: inconstancy, boredom, and anxiety. The world has changed drastically since Pascal's times, but the state of mankind is more or less the same. In the moral realm there is never anything new. Men may be less inconstant and boredom may have been relieved a bit since the seventeenth century, but these two states or elements of life are still with us. It's the degree of intensity that varies from one generation to another.

If behaviorists can be believed, there's more anxiety nowadays than ever before. But peace of mind is what we all want—the composure of an untroubled soul. Peace of mind—not torpor, not mindless inertia, but the tranquillity of a heart at rest. This is what everybody wants. But where to find it, that's the question.

Peace of mind depends upon knowledge. Take a mother whose small son is missing. The mother imagines unimaginable things and is nearly frantic with anxiety. Then she learns that the boy was never in danger; he had simply wandered over to Grandma's house and was napping after eating a dozen cookies. With knowledge came peace of mind. She is greatly relieved, and even willing to forgive Junior for having left the yard without telling her.

Peace of mind about our souls also depends upon knowledge. If we didn't know that God loves us and is willing to save us, we'd *never* have real peace. We would spend our lives wondering whether we'd make it to Heaven, and the uncertainty would destroy any possibility of peace of mind.

Just knowing that God loves you isn't enough, of course. You must also believe certain truths. As St. Paul explained it, "If you confess with your mouth, 'Jesus is Lord,' and believe in your heart that God raised him from the dead, you will be saved" (Romans 10:9). That's a great statement! Many souls have confessed Jesus as Lord, believing in their hearts that God has raised him from the dead, and they are truly saved. Yet, they have no peace of mind. The trouble is, not all of them know that there is nothing more they can or need to do to be saved. So they sweat it out for the rest of their lives, wondering if their good deeds outweigh their bad ones. They are saved, but they are miserable; they have no peace of mind.

Where can they find such peace? In the Bible! By learning what God says about salvation! Peace of mind depends upon knowing God's Word and, of course, faith to believe it. There is another element too—willingness to accept God's Word. Dante expressed it beautifully in his *Divine Comedy.* "And in His will is our peace," Dante wrote (*Paradiso,* Canto III, 85). Peace of mind belongs to the person who, knowing God's Word, believes it and accepts it for himself. As Isaiah said in prayer, "You will keep in perfect peace him whose mind is steadfast, because he trusts in you" (Isaiah 26:3).

The Apostle Paul said, "Since we have been justified by faith, we have peace with God" (Romans 5:1). If we have peace with God, what's left to keep our minds unsettled? If we have peace with God, we may also have peace of mind. Nothing could be more senseless than to go through life wondering, when God has said all that need be said about the subject.

The testimony of millions is that they have found peace in trusting God. A number of hymns express this beautifully. Take that great hymn which is sung to the tune of Finlandia: "Be still my soul: the Lord is on thy side; / Bear patiently the cross of grief or pain; / Leave to thy God to order and provide; / In every change he faithful will remain. / Be still my soul: thy best, thy heavenly Friend / Through thorny ways leads to a joyful end."

Those who know that God is on their side can indeed hush their souls. Like Edward Bickersteth, they find peace, perfect peace. His hymn gives his personal testimony:

Peace, perfect peace, in this dark world of sin?
The blood of Jesus whispers peace within.

Peace, perfect peace, the gift of God within;
It cometh not til grace hath conquered sin.

Peace, perfect peace, by thronging duties pressed?
To do the will of Jesus, this is rest.

Peace, perfect peace, with loved ones far away?
In Jesus' keeping we are safe, and they.

Peace, perfect peace, our future all unknown?
Jesus we know, and he is on the throne.

That just about says it all—a poet's statement of biblical truth. Knowing the Lord and trusting him brings real peace to every troubled heart.

This is what Paul meant when he urged his friends to pray, not to fret. "Do not be anxious about anything," he says, meaning, don't let a battle rage in your soul. Instead, "in everything by prayer and petition, with thanksgiving, present your requests to God. And the peace of God, which transcends all understanding, will guard your hearts and your minds in Christ Jesus" (Philippians 4:6, 7).

If you don't know the Lord, you can't find real peace. You may stumble onto plenty of substitutes, no doubt, but not the real thing. So the thing to do now is to trust him. Come to Jesus Christ, believing what he says and opening your life to him. Then you will experience and discover the meaning of inner peace.

Where does peace of mind come from? In a sense, it comes from without—from the Book in which God's Word is enshrined. But in another sense, it comes from within. It is the state of mind of the person who, knowing God's Word and believing it, gives up his senseless anxieties. Instead, he trusts God and in doing so, is at peace.

If anyone is in Christ, he is a new creation; the old has gone, the new has come! (2 Corinthians 5:17)

As Jesus was walking beside the Sea of Galilee, he saw two brothers, Simon called Peter and his brother Andrew. They were casting a net into the lake, for they were fishermen. "Come, follow me," Jesus said, "and I will make you fishers of men." At once they left their nets and followed him. (Matthew 4:18-20)

Just as you received Christ Jesus as Lord, continue to live in him. (Colossians 2:6)

We are God's workmanship, created in Christ Jesus to do good works, which God prepared in advance for us to do. (Ephesians 2:10)

4/WHAT DOES IT MEAN TO BE A CHRISTIAN?

Terms like "Christian," "born again," and "believer" are frequently used but not always understood. Even those who have received Christ as Savior don't always understand what it really means to be and live as a Christian.

What is a real Christian?

It's odd, but the Bible doesn't really give a definition of a Christian. It says a lot about Christians, so that the genuine article should be easily recognized, but it doesn't give a concise definition.

The question is complicated by the fact that there are both real and bogus Christians, though many of the false Christians are not consciously so. There are several uses for the one word. For example, the word *Christian* is used linguistically to designate virtually everyone who is born in a so-called "Christian" country, except of course those who may be Jewish or Moslem or Buddhist or a member of some other persuasion. We have this habit of speaking of races and cultures in religious terms, so that Europeans are Christians and Arabs are Moslems. Non-Arabs living in Arab lands are usually called Christians, whether they have ever been to church or not. They may use the name only to swear, yet they are considered Christians. But by biblical definitions they are not Christians at all.

It may be helpful to turn to the three places in the New Testament where the word *Christian* appears and see why this word was used.

The first of these is in Acts 11:26, where we find the simple statement, "The disciples were first called Christians at Antioch." That's not much help, but in the same paragraph it tells us what or whom the disciples were disciples of. Believers came to Antioch and preached the good news of the Lord Jesus (verse 20). The next verse says that those who believed turned to the Lord, and a few lines later we read that Barnabas came to Antioch and encouraged the disciples to remain true to the Lord, after which it says that multitudes were brought to the Lord and called Christians.

Well, those statements are clues. Did you catch the emphasis on the Lord? The message was about him; believers were brought to him and encouraged to remain true to him. So maybe a good definition of a Christian is a person who believes the message about Christ, comes to him (spiritually speaking, of course), and remains loyal and true to him.

It is interesting that the term *Christian* was first used by non-Christians to designate the followers of Jesus Christ. As it happened, the word was not meant to be a compliment.

There is another passage in Acts where the word *Christian* is also found, in chapter 26. A king had a special hearing of the gospel as preached by the Apostle Paul. What did Paul talk about? About Christ—especially his sufferings, death, and resurrection from the dead. Paul also talked about repentance and then urged the king to believe. That was when the king protested that Paul was trying to make a Christian out of him. So King Agrippa thought he knew what a Christian was—a man who believed the message about Jesus Christ and repented of his sins.

In the only other place in the Bible where the word *Christian* is used, Peter spoke of suffering as a Christian (1 Peter 4:16). "If you suffer as a Christian," he said, "do not be ashamed, but praise God that you bear that name." Peter thought it was an honor to be called a Christian.

To grasp Peter's meaning in its fullness you have to read the entire epistle, or at least the chapter. For Peter, Christians were believers who had been redeemed by the precious blood of Christ and were fully committed to him. If following him meant suffering for his name's sake, so be it. What mattered was accepting the will of God for them as Christ's disciples.

Paul frequently spoke of believers as those who belong to Christ; that's what it means to be a Christian (see 1 Corinthians 3:23; 7:23;

2 Corinthians 10:7; Galatians 3:29). A real Christian is one who consciously surrenders himself to Christ, and then proves it by the life he lives. St. Paul and Peter both liked to insist that real Christians were bought with a price (1 Corinthians 7:23; 1 Peter 1:18, 19); consequently, the reality of their faith in Christ would reveal itself in sober conduct.

When you put together all the passages in the Bible on this subject, you have to conclude that a Christian is one who, like those early believers in Antioch, turns to the Lord with a repentant heart, believes the gospel, and spends the rest of his life quietly proving it by his works.

One thing is certain—it is not good enough just to say, "Lord, Lord." A true Christian will give evidence in his life of an irrevocable commitment to Jesus Christ.

What do you have to do to become a Christian?

It depends upon the definition of *Christian*. If a Christian is just anyone who is born in a so-called "Christian" country, then you don't have to do anything; it was done for you when you were born, or perhaps later when you were baptized—if that's your definition of a Christian. The rub is, those definitions won't work. The Bible doesn't give a concise definition of *Christian*, but rather describes what this means so it can be recognized. A genuine Christian is one who has put his trust in Christ. He has committed himself to Jesus Christ; he has opened his heart to Christ.

What do you have to do to become *that* kind of Christian?

In a sense, not much; all you have to do is believe the gospel, or, to be more precise, believe in Jesus. Here's a plain statement taken from the Gospel According to John: "For God so loved the world that he gave his one and only Son, that whoever believes in him shall not perish but have eternal life" (John 3:16). Did you get that? Whoever believes in God's Son receives everlasting life! That's an astonishing offer.

It's hard for us to accept this as true; we seem psychologically incapable of believing that God really means it—that he gives us eternal life for simply believing. But the Bible emphasizes the term.

For example, in that same passage the speaker (who was probably Jesus himself) said that God "did not send his Son into the world to condemn the world, but to save the world through him. Whoever believes in him is not condemned. . . ."

The apostles certainly understood the importance of belief in Jesus. Peter summed it up neatly when he said, "All the prophets testify about him [Christ] that everyone who believes in him receives forgiveness of sins through his name" (Acts 10:43). Paul said the same thing. In his first recorded sermon he said that "through him [Jesus] everyone who believes is justified . . ." (Acts 13:39), and he never changed his message.

There is another dimension to this truth: belief as used in the Bible is not just mental assent to a few pious propositions; it is commitment, and it comes with repentance. In Antioch, where Christ's followers were first called Christians, the description of their conversion is significant. A great number of people believed, the Bible says, and they "turned to the Lord" (see Acts 11:21). The NIV says they "were brought to the Lord" (verse 24), so that they became Christ's disciples—i.e., his followers (verse 26).

Another point to be underlined is that you have to believe certain truths. Firm convictions, unshakable beliefs do no good at all if they are misdirected. To become a Christian you have to believe clearly stated facts, no ifs and buts about it. Here's how Paul explained it:

> If you confess with your mouth, "Jesus is Lord," and believe in your heart that God raised him from the dead, you will be saved. (Romans 10:9)

So there it is: turn to the Lord, believing the facts of the gospel about him, and confessing sincerely that Jesus is Lord. That's how to become a Christian.

Does baptism bring us salvation?

In Paul's last letter from prison he urged his younger friend, Timothy, to handle the word of truth accurately (2 Timothy 2:15).

Paul wrote in Greek, of course, and the Greek word he used means "to cut straight," as a furrow or a stone being shaped for a building. The Greek scholar A. T. Robertson thinks that Paul, who made his living making tents, was thinking of the care he took in cutting the camel-hair cloth used to make tents. Cut it straight, he says; don't turn out crazy-quilt pattern tents.

Careful handling of the word of truth (i.e., the Bible) would spare us much of the crazy-quilt theologies that confuse Christians and divide churches. Nearly every Bible teacher assumes, of course, that he personally is handling the Bible accurately; it's the other chap whose teaching is awry. No doubt this problem will persist until the Lord returns.

Even so, it seems to me that *careful* reading of a sometimes controversial text in Mark's Gospel (as well as other passages dealing with baptism) should correct the notion that baptism is essential to salvation.

Here is Mark's text about which there is some confusion: "And he (that is, Jesus) said to them, 'Go into all the world and preach the good news to all creation. Whoever believes and is baptized will be saved, but whoever does not believe will be condemned'" (Mark 16:15, 16).

At first glance the text *seems* to say that baptism is essential, that without it one cannot be saved. Careful reading corrects that notion. How? By describing the people who are condemned. Are they those who don't accept baptism? No; the condemned are those who do not "believe." Nobody is "condemned" because he is not baptized, or was baptized incorrectly. The condemned are unbelievers.

The interpretation of the passage does not minimize the importance of baptism; it gives it its rightful place—as an act of obedience to Christ in whom one professes faith. The Lord expects believers to be baptized, even as he expects (or *wants*) believers to obey *all* his commandments. However, by adding that those who disbelieve are condemned, he tries to protect us from the error of thinking that baptism saves. Salvation is by faith alone (see John 3:18, 36; Ephesians 2:8, 9).

One other truth is implied in this passage: even baptized people may be eternally condemned. Anyone can submit to a rite, for any of a variety of motives. Maybe you were baptized in infancy, but grew up unbelieving. You stand condemned. Maybe you were baptized as an adolescent—because your friends were being baptized. If you are unbelieving, you stand condemned—which is frightening to contemplate.

Another baptism text, Acts 2:38, gives Peter's reply to the question put to him by his listeners in Jerusalem. Here's what it says: "Repent, and be baptized in the name of Jesus Christ so that your sins may be forgiven. And you will receive the gift of the Holy Spirit." Does this passage teach baptismal regeneration? The answer is no. Bearing in mind the many passages that proclaim salvation through faith alone, Thomas Walker remarks correctly that Peter's listeners were to be baptized

> as the sign and token that they accepted Jesus Christ as their Savior and Lord. Repentance must be followed by the definite acceptance of Christ, and baptism is the divinely appointed sacrament in which such faith is publicly expressed.

Remission for sins—that is, pardon—does not follow a merely external rite; it is conferred upon those who put their trust in Jesus.

Consider also 1 Peter 3:21, which reads as follows: ". . . baptism that now saves you also—not the removal of dirt from the body but the pledge of a good conscience toward God. It saves you by the resurrection of Jesus Christ. . . ." Does baptism save? Passages like this one *seem* to say it does, which raises these questions: How does it save, and what does it save from?

The answer can be found only by studying the verses that immediately precede the reference to baptism. Peter speaks of the ark (verse 20)—the bargelike thing built by Noah—in which eight persons were saved from death during the great flood. The ark was a symbol. In fact, the whole scene was symbolic, the waters representing death, and the ark the means whereby Noah and his family passed safely through that judgment. Thus, the ark portrays Christ, who saves all who trust in him and are "in him," as Paul would say.

What is the connection between this and baptism? Baptism is also a symbol; it symbolizes a believer's union with Christ in his death. Christ really died; he passed through the waters of death. Through faith, we believers are united to him, linked with him in a union so close that God regards us as having died with Christ. We didn't die, of course. Here we are, nearly 2,000 years after the event. Nevertheless, God views us through Christ, so to speak. Baptism symbolizes this death with which we are credited. In this sense, it saves us.

We must read the passage carefully. If we do, we'll see that a good part of it is parenthetical. Remove that and the passage reads this way: ". . . baptism now saves you . . . by the resurrection of Jesus Christ."

Ah, there's the real ground and source of salvation—Jesus Christ, put to death in the flesh, but raised from the dead and made Lord and Savior of all who trust him.

So you see, he who has believed and has been baptized will be saved. If you have neither believed nor been baptized, what's keeping you from it?

What is the purpose or meaning of Christian baptism?

What is baptism?

Many Christians believe that baptism commemorates the coming of the Holy Spirit. This view is not without biblical support. For example, in 1 Corinthians 12:13 we read that "we were all baptized by one Spirit into one body . . . and we were all given the one Spirit to drink." This is Paul's explanation of the events that took place in Jerusalem shortly after our Lord's ascension. Peter explained the phenomena—that is, the sound of a gale blowing through the house, followed by speech in a variety of languages which the speakers had never studied—as evidence of fulfillment of God's promise to send his Holy Spirit. Said Peter, "(The Father) has poured out what you now see and hear" (Acts 2:33).

Did you catch that word "poured"? It explains the practice of pouring or sprinkling. For those who believe that baptism dramatized the coming of the Holy Spirit, pouring or sprinkling are proper modes of baptism. Certain passages, such as those that say that thousands were baptized in one day, seem to support that view (for example, see Acts 2:41).

Many other Christians, on the other hand, believe that baptism portrays our union with Christ in his death, burial, and resurrection. In support of this view, they cite passages such as Romans 6:4—"We were therefore buried with him through baptism into death. . . ." Accordingly, they baptize by immersion—which is the proper mode if the act is intended to dramatize burial (Colossians 2:12; cf. 1 Peter 3:20, 21).

In the Bible the verb "to baptize" is always used in the passive voice. Nobody is ever told to baptize himself; he is told, instead, to be baptized—necessarily by someone else, who acts as God's representative. What this means is that baptism is primarily "God's act toward us, not ours toward God" (W. H. Griffith Thomas, *The Catholic Faith,* page 161).

Nowhere in the New Testament is baptism clearly explained. Even passages such as Romans 6, with its seemingly clear references to baptism, does not do so; the passage merely cites baptism to reinforce the idea of practical holiness. The reason why the New Testament does not explain baptism may be that the early disciples, being Jews, were familiar with the rite and understood its underlying meaning. Certainly the Jews used water in significant ceremonies, such as the consecration of the high priest to the priesthood, and the Levites to their service in the Tabernacle (cf. Exodus 29:1, 4; Numbers 8:7; Hebrews 9:10).

What was the purpose in those ancient washings or baptisms? There were two ideas: a symbolic purification and designation for service. In the New Testament the emphasis seems to be on the second of the two ideas. Have you ever noticed the little Greek preposition that often follows the word "baptize"? It is translated variously "in," "into," "unto," and "for." It means "with a view to," and indicates the purpose of the baptism. For example, Paul says that ancient Israel had been baptized "into Moses," meaning that its baptism was with a view to following Moses out of Egypt (1 Corinthians 10:2, cf. Acts 19:3).

It boils down to this: baptism is an act of God—done, of course, by his representatives on earth—whereby he publicly marks out his people for union with himself through our Lord Jesus Christ. As Dr. Thomas says, "It is . . . a witness of God's act and attitude of condescending mercy in Christ and a pledge of his grace toward us . . ." (page 163).

The human response to baptism takes two forms: the duty to baptize converts, and the duty of converts to accept baptism. God expects new Christians to receive baptism.

This is emphasized in Mark's version of the Great Commission. Whereas Matthew remembers what the Lord said to the apostles, commissioning them to make disciples and baptize them, Mark remembers what he said about the disciples themselves. Here is Mark's account of the Great Commission (16:15, 16):

> Go into all the world and preach the good news to all creation. Whoever believes and is baptized will be saved; but whoever does not believe will be condemned.

Did you catch what Mark says? Not, "go . . . and make disciples, baptizing them," but "whoever believes and is baptized will be saved." Instead of a command, he gives a description of new Christians: they believe, and they receive baptism.

Does this mean that baptism is essential to salvation? The answer is no. Nevertheless, baptism is part of the Great Commission; preachers are commanded to baptize new disciples, and new disciples are instructed to receive baptism.

In the first century, Christians took this command seriously. Acts tells us that as many as heard the gospel and believed were baptized, evidently without delay. There is no instance of any believer either refusing baptism or showing indifference to it. When the apostles preached the gospel, they told their listeners that they should be baptized—not to save their souls, but in obedience to their new Lord. And without exception, converts were baptized.

What this means for us today should be obvious. If we have trusted Christ, whether in a church building or elsewhere, we should take the first step asked of believers: baptism in the name of the Father and the Son and the Holy Spirit.

Very few converts understand baptism at the time they experience it. For them, it is enough to know that Christ commands it. At the time, obedience is uppermost in their minds. Later some think about its meaning.

In accepting baptism, we give testimony. Our testimony as Christians is certainly not limited to baptism; in fact, the whole of our Christian life is a confession of Christ. Nevertheless, in baptism we make a special confession: we acknowledge our union with Christ, especially in his death, burial, and resurrection.

Acknowledge is too weak a word; we *dramatize* our union with

Christ. This is true whether we are sprinkled or immersed. In the one case, sprinkling or pouring is intended to portray the coming of the Holy Spirit, who unites us to Christ and secures for us the values of his atoning death. In the other, the mode—immersion—simulates burial. As Paul says, we are "buried with (Christ) through baptism" (Romans 6:4). We don't really die, and we aren't really buried, and we don't really rise again. We play-act, so to speak. But we do it seriously, in this way testifying to our union with Christ in and through his atoning death.

The effect of this is what may be termed moral and ethical awareness. In reply to the suggestion that free salvation permits one to sin to his heart's content, Paul appealed to the experience of baptism. Phillips translates the passage in this way:

> We, who have died to sin—how could we live in sin a moment longer? Have you forgotten that all of us who were baptised into Jesus Christ were, by that very action, sharing in his death? We were dead and buried with him in baptism, so that just as he was raised from the dead by that splendid revelation of the Father's power so we too might rise to life on a new plane altogether. (Romans 6:2-4)

Baptism, then, witnesses to our commitment to holiness. On the divine side, it is God's gift to us, his designation of us as united to him. On the human side, it is evidence of commitment; we portray in dramatic form our union with Christ in his death, burial, and resurrection and our acceptance of the implications.

We experience the mere likeness of what Christ experienced in reality. We act out the death he actually suffered. In this way we confess that we should have been the victims, but that he died for us. Now, forever united to him through faith, we pledge our fealty to him and say that we wish to live "on a new plane altogether," as Christ's people.

This is what baptism means to us.

If a person was baptized by sprinkling, is his baptism valid?

Behind this question is the assumption that the scriptural mode of baptism is immersion. Many Christians disagree; they would formulate the question to ask whether baptism by immersion is valid. So we should thrash out the question of the meaning of baptism and the mode best suited to express that meaning. But that would still leave unsettled the question of validity, for the validity of one's baptism does not depend upon the method used, whether one was sprinkled or immersed. It depends upon one's subsequent manner of life.

This is the approach the Apostle Paul takes. He doesn't bother to explain baptism; he assumes that his readers understand it. He reminds them, however, that baptism and Christian conduct are very closely related. A familiar passage on the subject is Romans 6, where Paul answers those who say that salvation on the basis of faith alone is an invitation to sin. "Not at all!" he says. "Have you forgotten your baptism?" In the discussion that follows, Paul shows how baptism is a dramatization of every Christian's union with Christ. Did Christ die? Well, the values of his death are transferred to Christians. Was he buried, and did he rise again? So has every true believer. In his case, death was real; in ours, it is "spiritual"—that is, charged to our credit in virtue of our association with him.

Baptism symbolizes this; it is a personal dramatization of the death, burial, and resurrection which Jesus Christ experienced in fact, and which Christians experience in association with him. The point Paul makes in Romans 6 is that a life of sin is incompatible with all which baptism symbolizes. Baptism itself may be a kind of mock death, burial, and resurrection, but the truths it symbolizes are real. Christians are indeed united to Christ, and for this reason they may not live sloppy, careless lives of sin.

Their baptism is a public acknowledgment of this great truth. Obviously, then, the validity of one's baptism is confirmed by his behavior. Those who live as do non-Christians show by their lives that their baptism—whether they were sprinkled or immersed—was an empty ceremony. It did nothing for them but get them wet.

Is Christianity all repentance and self-denial, or can Christians really enjoy life?

Horace was a Roman poet (65-68 B.C.) who advised a friend in a letter to "receive . . . with a thankful hand" whatever prosperous hour Providence might bestow upon him, "and defer not the enjoyment of the comforts of life." What do Christians enjoy most in life?

For all of us, no doubt, Christian or non-Christian, achievement brings more joy than anything else. *Achievement* may seem too pretentious a word, but it doesn't necessarily mean grand accomplishments. Getting what you're after—that's what I mean.

For us Christians it's important to go after the right things. The Apostle Paul said we make it our ambition in life to please God (2 Corinthians 5:9). Anything less than that would be ultimately disappointing. Meanwhile, living for God brings joy into one's life. Even thinking about God brings joy, strange though that may sound to an unbeliever or a person whose only joys are purely physical. As Paul said, "we also rejoice in God" (Romans 5:11). But there's no sense trying to explain it to one who has never experienced it; he wouldn't understand. This kind of joy comes from the Holy Spirit (Romans 14:17; Galatians 5:22).

Maybe a non-Christian *can* understand the joy we have in the companionship of good friends. Paul wrote that he longed to see his friends in a town called Philippi. He said they were his joy (Philippians 4:1), and he rejoiced because of their concern for him (4:10), and because of their spiritual vitality in general. Paul said he knew they, in turn, would have joy when Epaphroditus visited them (2:25ff.). The great apostle's writings frequently mention his profound satisfaction in visiting his friends, or just hearing that they are growing in spiritual strength.

The Apostle John felt the same way. He wrote that he had no greater joy than to hear that his friends in the family of God were walking in the truth (3 John 4). What gave him joy was not just their pleasing personalities; it was the lives which they lived in obedience to the will of God.

That about says it all: we Christians joy in God, and we enjoy each other's company more than anything else on the purely human level. We *can* enjoy the comforts of life, but they aren't essential. Paul learned to be content with very little; whether full or hungry, he was content, because he knew his circumstances were not out of God's control (Philippians 4:10ff.). What is essential for us to enjoy life is the assurance that we are walking in obedience to God's Word. If so, we will have a concern for our brothers and sisters in the Lord, and when we hear that they are okay or when we see them, we'll be full of real joy. There's really nothing sweeter than being with those who love the Lord. They are the excellent of the earth, and their company brings joy.

What does it cost to be a disciple of Jesus Christ?

When Saul of Tarsus became a Christian, his entire outlook on life was radically changed. He even changed his name, dropping an honored Hebrew name for an insignificant Greek equivalent. Not that he was ashamed of his Jewishness; anti-Semitism was rare in those days, and when a colonel in the Roman Army asked him if he were an Egyptian, Paul corrected him quietly. "I am a Jew," he said (Acts 21:39). He was grateful for the benefits his birth had conferred upon him.

As a Christian, however, he was willing to forgo natural advantages. He had found something of surpassing value, and compared to that, what he had once highly esteemed he could now regard as rubbish. What he had found was not a thing, or an abstraction such as pride of birth; it—if you will permit the grammar—was a Person. He had found Jesus Christ, and knowing Christ as Lord made everything else pale into insignificance by comparison.

Paul spoke of the "surpassing greatness of knowing Christ Jesus my Lord" (Philippians 3:8). The knowledge of Christ was more excellent than any earthly advantage. Consequently, Paul was willing to pay whatever price might be asked for the privilege of knowing Christ. In his case, the cost was quite high. It included pride of birth and pride of accomplishment in the religion of his ancestors and no doubt other losses that Paul did not mention. Some Bible students believe that his statement that he had suffered the loss of "all things" (Philippians 3:8) implied that his family had disowned him. Knowing Christ had wiped out both ancestral and material advantages.

So the price was high, but in Paul's case it had to be paid. The very nature of the new relationship he found when he became a Christian undermined the basis for pride in former relationships. Paul himself wrote to Christians in Galatia that "there is neither Jew nor Greek . . . for you are all one in Christ Jesus" (Galatians 3:28). For Christians, racial distinctions do not exist—not, at least, as a source of pride or a claim to special advantage before God. Paul's pride of birth had to go.

Following Christ always exacts a price, and Jesus never concealed that fact. He warned volunteers that "Foxes have holes, and the birds of the air have nests . . ." in contrast to him who at that time had no home of his own (Matthew 8:20). He spoke of devotion to himself in terms of loss—loss of family, even loss of life (cf. Matt. 10:37-39). Devotion to Christ means taking up a cross. What that means was clearly understood by Paul who said it meant that the world was dead to him (cf. Galatians 6:14); he wrote it off as a personal loss.

Did it hurt? At first, perhaps. But the better he knew his Lord, the easier it was to regard those former treasures as mere rubbish. Compared to knowing Christ Jesus as Lord, the best the world has to offer is only garbage.

Does prayer really work?

No, prayer does not work; it is not a device or method calculated to produce results. However, prayer gets results, since it is the means whereby we ask God for what we need. Not that we tell him what he doesn't already know. In the Sermon on the Mount our Lord assures us that we don't have to recite repetitious prayers. In fact, he commands us to avoid that sort of thing, for—he explains—"your Father knows what you need" (Matthew 6:8). Then he tells us how to pray: "Our Father in heaven, hallowed be your name. . . ," etc. If he knows what we need without our asking, why bother him? Why pray?

The answer is, some of God's promises are conditional, and one of the chief conditions is that we ask. In the same sermon our Lord said, "Ask and it will be given to you" (Matthew 7:7). Later he said, "I will do whatever you ask in my name" (John 14:13). And, "My Father will give whatever you ask in my name" (John 16:23). There is also the incident of the healing of a couple of blind men, on which occasion Jesus said, "According to your faith will it be done to you" (Matthew 9:29). What he meant was that asking must be done in faith. So there are two conditions: asking, and faith in God.

That this is precisely what Jesus meant is plain from a comment on these matters by James. "You do not have," he said to some of his fellow-Christians, "because you do not ask God" (James 4:2). No asking, no receiving—that's the way it is in the Christian life. James also emphasized the need of asking in faith for the right things— which do not include unnecessary things that just make life softer (verse 3).

Those who abide in Christ and keep his words (John 15:7) usually ask in faith for the things God wants to give them. Inevitably they get what they ask for in prayer. But it isn't a case of prayers that work; it is a matter of having to do with a God who answers prayer. It is God who "works," not the prayers.

If you saw someone heading in the wrong direction, would you help him? Why get involved?

I'm not sure what I *would* do, but I know what I *should* do: I should help him or her. Not because I'm a nice guy or naturally disposed to helping people in trouble, but because God demands it of me, and will be satisfied with nothing less.

Modern indifference to the plight of people in trouble is wrong— dead wrong. Jesus, whom we Christians call Lord, once answered a question about the commandments in such a way as to emphasize the importance of concern for others. The greatest commandment demands love to God, but the second requires love for your neighbor. "Love your neighbor as yourself," he said (Matthew 22:39).

What he meant by love for neighbors was illustrated in his own parable of the good Samaritan (Luke 10:30-35), and was also explained by Paul (Romans 13:8ff.) and James (2:8ff.; 4:17). The good Samaritan saw a man who had been mugged and left half-dead on a dangerous highway. He stopped to help, though a couple of others had passed by without stopping. The Samaritan got involved—to the extent of taking the injured man to the hospital, so to speak. It took time, and it cost him a bundle to do it. But our Lord commended him for it, then said to his listeners and to us, "Go and do likewise."

The Apostle Paul underlined the negative side of the commandment. He said, "Love does no harm to its neighbor" (Romans 13:10). But he also said that love prompts a person to serve his neighbor (Galatians 5:13, 14). In other words, get involved. This is precisely what James meant when he scoffed at the piousness of those who say sweet things to people in trouble without lifting a finger to help them: "If a fellow man or woman has no clothes to wear and nothing to eat, and one of you say 'Good luck to you, I hope you'll keep warm and find enough to eat,' and yet give them nothing to meet their physical needs, what on earth is the good of that?" (James 2:14ff., *Phillips*).

James said in effect that Christians who mean business with God get involved. There's no excuse for standing aloof. In fact, James went so far as to say that "if a man knows what is right and fails to do it, his failure is a real sin" (4:17, *Phillips*). If we don't get involved, we're guilty of sin.

All Scripture is God-breathed and is useful for teaching, rebuking, correcting and training in righteousness, so that the man of God may be thoroughly equipped for every good work. (2 Timothy 3:16, 17)

The law of the Lord is perfect, reviving the soul. The statutes of the Lord are trustworthy, making wise the simple. The precepts of the Lord are right, giving joy to the heart. The commands of the Lord are radiant, giving light to the eyes. The fear of the Lord is pure, enduring forever. The ordinances of the Lord are sure and altogether righteous. They are more precious than gold, than much pure gold; they are sweeter than honey, than honey from the comb. By them is your servant warned; in keeping them there is great reward. (Psalm 19:7-11)

"All men are like grass, and all their glory is like the flowers of the field; the grass withers and the flowers fall, but the word of the Lord stands forever." (1 Peter 1:24, 25)

It is impossible for God to lie. (Hebrews 6:18)

5/CAN I TRUST WHAT THE BIBLE SAYS?

The Bible makes some pretty astounding claims and offers much comfort and strength for our lives, if we can just be confident that it speaks truly.

Who wrote the Bible?

Who wrote the Bible? When was it written, and in what language?

Taking these questions in reverse order, it can be stated at the outset that the documents that comprise our Bible were originally written in either of two languages: Hebrew for the Old Testament documents, and Greek for the New Testament. To a lesser extent, Aramaic was used, though none of the documents was composed entirely in that language. When Bible students refer to the "original documents," they are speaking of writings in Hebrew or Greek. The English Bible is a translation.

When was the Bible written? The answer is, long before the publication of the first English language Bible! The Bible is really a collection of books that were written over a 1,600-year span. From the writing of the first book, or document, in the collection to the writing of the last, a millenium and a half passed, during which as many as sixty generations of people were born and died. Obviously the Bible was not written in the same way as are most books—by an author or, in some cases, a team of authors who finish the job within their lifetime.

The Bible was written by many authors. More than forty men contributed to the collection called the Bible. The first few books were probably written by Moses, and the last by the Apostle John. For a list of others who wrote the Bible, check the table of contents in any copy. This won't give all the names, since some of the books were written anonymously. (Maybe not anonymously; when they first appeared readers may have known the names of the authors. But we don't know them. Who wrote First Kings? We don't know. And we're not even certain that Malachi wrote the book by that name. Why not? Because Malachi isn't really a name; it is a word meaning "messenger." Thus, it may be a pseudonym.)

It doesn't matter. What matters is that in spite of the immense span of time—1,600 years—and the variety of authors—more than forty—the Bible is a book. It is not a library; it is a single volume remarkable for its unity. It should also be said that the unity of theme in the Bible—its witness to Christ—is a powerful proof of its supernatural origin. Peter explains the matter when he says that "men spoke from God as they were carried along by the Holy Spirit" (2 Peter 1:21). God himself is the source of the Scriptures; otherwise, there would not be—indeed, could not be—the remarkable unity the Bible exhibits. The Bible is God's Book, his gift to us.

Is reading any great religious document as helpful as reading the Bible?

At lunch one day a friend told me that an acquaintance of his had just changed churches for the strangest reason. For weeks prior to the decision the Sunday morning services in that man's church had been made an occasion for experiments. The traditional sermon was regarded as passé, an affliction to which moderns could not submit. "Dialogue" and other innovative things were in. The acquaintance endured it quietly, hoping that things would improve. They didn't; instead, they worsened. The breaking point came when a lesson in the practice of yoga was scheduled for the Sunday morning service. He decided to switch churches. Not that he had anything against yoga or objected to people standing on their heads; he just felt that Sunday morning was not the time for it, nor a Christian church the place for it.

He was right, of course. Sunday is in a special sense "the Lord's day," and it would take a skillful talker to persuade most of us that pursuits which may be okay six days a week are equally appropriate on Sundays. Demosthenes himself could not persuade us that yoga was *ever* appropriate in church, much less on Sunday. No matter how watered-down imported versions may be, it remains true that yoga is essentially Hindu and therefore utterly inappropriate in a Christian church.

Besides, the purpose of a gathering of Christians is for the study of the Word of God and its application to life. There are other purposes, to be sure, such as collective prayer and praise and worship of God, and fellowship with each other as Christians. But the Bible is central; without reference to it none of the exercises listed here would be meaningful. The Bible tells us who God is, what he is like, how to worship him, why to praise and thank him, how to pray, why the company of other Christians is both desirable and helpful, and teaches us how to live as Christians. A gathering of Christians that pays no attention to the Scriptures is unthinkable.

This doesn't mean that Christians must turn every occasion into a Bible reading. Christians also need to socialize. But we're talking about church, the place where Christians meet for the specific purposes just mentioned. In church, whether it be a huge granite pile, a frame building with a steeple, a storefront church, or a church so small the Christians meet in their homes, the reading of the Scriptures is or should be central. In one of the three New Testament documents called the pastoral epistles (because they tell Timothy and Titus how to tend the flock of God), Paul urges Timothy to devote himself "to the public reading of Scripture, to preaching and to teaching" (1 Timothy 4:13).

In another passage he emphasizes the value of the Scriptures and their profound effect on all who listen and obey. The Scriptures are able to make a person "wise for salvation through faith in Christ Jesus." Moreover, Scripture, being "God-breathed," is "useful for teaching, rebuking, correcting and training in righteousness, so that the man of God may be thoroughly equipped for every good work" (2 Timothy 3:15-17).

There is no substitute for the Bible. Nothing else can train in righteousness and equip the man of God for every good work. Certainly not yoga! We dare not substitute every notion that comes along for the preaching and teaching of what is no less than the Word of God!

Why do Christians believe the Bible?

The Apostle Peter says that we Christians ought to be able to defend the reason for the hope that is in us (1 Peter 3:15). He means that we should know not only what we believe, but why. For most of us, the immediate answer is that we believe what the Bible tells us, and we believe it because it is the Bible that says it. In the minds of nonbelievers, however, that is circular reasoning and therefore unconvincing.

What they don't know is that Christians believe the Bible to be the infallible, inerrant Word of God. When this truth is understood, it is fairly clear that Christians don't think in circles; it makes sense to say that we believe what the Bible says, and we believe it because it is the Bible that says it.

The real question is, *why* do we believe the Bible is the Word of God? This topic's importance can scarcely be overestimated because if the source of our theology is polluted, what shall we say about our theology? Or, to put it another way, if the Bible is not in fact what Christian people believe it to be—the Word of God—who cares what it says? Nobody, really.

The Bible is God's written revelation. Here is Dr. Clark Pinnock's definition of the biblical doctrine of the inspiration of the Scriptures:

> The Bible in its entirety is God's written Word to man, free of error in its original autographs, wholly reliable in history and doctrine. Its divine inspiration has rendered the book "infallible" (incapable of teaching deception) and "inerrant" (not liable to prove false or mistaken). Its inspiration is "plenary" (extending to all parts alike), "verbal" (including the actual language form), and "confluent" (product of two agents, human and divine). *Inspiration* involves *infallibility* as an essential property, and infallibility in turn implies inerrancy. . . . (*A Defense of Biblical Infallibility,* page 1)

Read that definition again and especially note the terms "infallible," "inerrant," "plenary," "verbal," and "confluent." These terms are crucial to an understanding of the biblical doctrine of the inspiration of the Scriptures.

Two observations come to mind. First, it should be obvious why we believers believe what we believe; we are convinced that the Bible is God's Word. Second, if we are right, nobody can safely ignore the Bible. This may be what one biblical writer had in mind when he said, "See to it that you do not refuse him who speaks. If they did not escape who refused him who warned them on earth, how much less will we, if we turn away from him who warns us from heaven?" (Hebrews 12:25).

Can we trust modern Bible translations as the Word of God?

When we talk about the Bible as the inspired Word of God, we talk about autographs and apographs. An *autograph* is an original manuscript; an *apograph* is a copy of it. Most people know that biblical autographs do not exist; they were lost centuries ago. However, we have plenty of apographs—i.e., copies of the originals. If the originals were divinely inspired, as we Christians believe, it follows that the copies are also divinely inspired. After all, the material is the same.

But is it? That is the question. The answer is yes. This is the opinion of specialists in the science of textual criticism. They believe that the text of the original manuscripts has been preserved virtually undamaged, which is remarkable considering the great antiquity of the writings. With respect to the reliability of the Old Testament, the concluding chapter of which was written some 400 years before Christ, a prominent scholar living in our times has this to say: ". . . the consonantal text of the Hebrew Bible which the Masseoretes edited had been handed down to their time (A.D. 500-900) with conspicuous fidelity over a period of nearly a thousand years" (F. F. Bruce, *The Books and the Parchments*, page 178).

Many scholars have noted the extreme care with which the Jewish scribes handled the text of their Scriptures. They counted every letter and mark. They devised systems calculated to prevent any scribal slip, and in this way oversaw the transmission of the Scriptures with the greatest accuracy imaginable.

What about the New Testament? F. F. Bruce says, "There is no body of ancient literature in the world which enjoys such a wealth of good textual attestation as the New Testament" (page 178). One reason for this is that about 13,000 copies of the original manuscripts exist. The more copies in existence, the greater the accuracy in determining the content of the originals. There are no more than five copies of any of Aristotle's writings, and the time lapse between his writing them and discovery of the copies now available was more than 1,400 years. Compare that with the 13,000 copies of New Testament writings, some of which were circulating between 200 and 300 years of their writing, and you can see how reliable the New Testament documents are. In ancient literature there is nothing that can be compared to it.

Furthermore, students of English literature soon discover that the texts of writers like Shakespeare are corrupted. As many as 100 different readings of Shakespeare's thirty-seven plays are available. In some places the meaning of the passage in question is seriously affected. And in the Melville Room in the Newberry Library, a collating machine was used in an attempt to determine the true reading of *Moby Dick,* which was written in 1851!

So the Bible is God's Book, divinely inspired and preserved through many centuries, a Book in which we may have confidence. Its words can illumine our minds, leading us to God through Jesus Christ our Lord.

Should the Bible be considered God's Word, or merely the writings of men?

C. S. Lewis was professor of medieval and Renaissance English literature at Cambridge University, a position which said something about his competence in literature. He was also a Christian and a writer of books about Christianity. In one of them he observed that "Our age has, indeed, coined the expression 'the Bible as literature.' " Lewis went on to say, "It is very generally implied that those who have rejected its theological pretensions nevertheless continue to enjoy it as a treasure-house of English prose." The question, of course, is whether the Bible can be considered merely good literature. C. S. Lewis insisted that he had never met anyone who, rejecting the Bible's religious claims, nevertheless remained a reader for its literary charms. "Unless the religious claims of the Bible are again acknowledged," he said, "its literary claims will . . . be given only 'mouth honor' and that decreasingly" (*They Asked for a Paper*, Chapter 2).

Should the Bible be viewed as literature, or as God's Word? It claims to be God's Word, not merely literature, not merely the writings of talented men. But other books have made the same claim. A crucial difference is that only the Bible has stood the tests of time and inquiry; every other pretender to divine inspiration has been quickly discredited.

A number of good reasons can be given for accepting the Bible's claim to be "God-breathed" (2 Timothy 3:16). Its very indestructibility is evidence of something unusual. Men have attacked the Bible frequently through the centuries and have predicted its end. But here we are in the space age, and at least twenty-five million copies are bought annually.

One could say quite a bit about the Bible's ideals, its ethical teachings, its integrity as a book notwithstanding the fact that it was written over a span of 1,600 years by about forty authors, and of course its prophetic element. So many implausible predictions have come true. For example, the prophet Jeremiah predicted that his people would be exiled for seventy years. Sure enough, seventy years later a pagan king released them, sending them back to Jerusalem. It can be demonstrated that Daniel predicted the actual week (some say day) of Christ's triumphal entry into Jerusalem some 400 years before it happened. Those whose presuppositions don't permit the miraculous have a terrible time explaining Daniel!

For my part, the final word about the Bible's claim to inspiration came from Jesus. He believed it was God's Word, and for me that's enough. Again and again he quoted the Old Testament, calling it Scripture which "cannot be broken" (John 10:35). When people asked him questions he referred them to the Scriptures. "What do the Scriptures say?" he asked them, or "Have you not read the Scriptures?" Jesus believed the Bible was God's Word, and he told his disciples that his own Holy Spirit would inspire the writing of the New Testament. Was he mistaken?

Christianity, of course, is based on the conviction that Jesus is Lord and on commitment to him. But who could believe in the Lordship of a man just as ignorant as everybody else? If he was mistaken in thinking the Old Testament was indeed the Word of God, how do we know he wasn't wrong on every other subject? And who can believe in such a person, or surrender his soul to him for safekeeping?

So the question really boils down to the character of Jesus Christ. Was he God in human form, or just a charismatic teacher? That's the real question, and how you answer it will determine where you spend eternity—in Heaven or in Hell.

As for me, I believe in Jesus Christ our Lord, and believing in him, I take his word on the veracity of the Bible.

Is the Bible reliable, even in the smallest details it records?

For many who like to read the Psalms and other reputedly literary passages in the Bible, the doctrine of inerrancy is like a bone in their throats; it troubles them very much indeed. In their thinking, God could not have inspired the writing of details which they regard as trivial. Passages such as Paul's request to Timothy to be sure to bring him the cloak he left in Troas seem too unimportant to have been inspired by God.

The objection is understandable. References to matters such as Timothy's stomach ailment, or the young man who followed Jesus into the Garden of Gethsemane and, caught by the guards, slipped out of his linen garment and ran away naked, seem to be a different class than doctrinal statements. However, this may not be the case at all. Who is to say which of the details included in Scripture are trivial, and which are essential?

The truth is, God chose to give us his Word in the form in which we have it. He did not choose to give us a series of essays or a long list of propositions. With a little thought, we can see the wisdom of God in using the form in which his Word takes shape. Instead of giving an abstract discussion of the sinfulness of deceit, he records episodes in which deceit revealed its essential nature. The story of David's sin with Bathsheba is a far more effective exposure of the folly of lust, adultery, and murder than the most brilliantly argued polemic.

Hence, it follows that the details such as David's afternoon nap, Bathsheba's bath, etc., are crucial to the story. They are parts of a literary unit, the recording of which was given in response to divine inspiration. To single out details as unessential is to do despite to the idea of inspiration; it reveals an unscriptural attitude toward the Scriptures.

The Bible's own attitude toward the supposedly unimportant details is clear from various passages. For example, Paul says that "everything that was written in the past (i.e., in the Old Testament) was written to teach us, so that through endurance and the encouragement of the Scriptures we might have hope" (Romans 15:4). In another place, speaking of events that happened during the Exodus, he says that "these things (i.e., the events in the wilderness) happened to them as examples and were written down as warnings for us . . ." (1 Corinthians 10:11).

Thus, Paul says plainly that matters of time and place and seemingly unimportant details are the fruit of inspiration. "All Scripture is inspired by God . . ." (2 Timothy 3:16, KJV). This does not mean that every statement is equally important, but it does mean that every statement is equally reliable. If the Bible says it happened, it happened, and it happened as described. The Bible is God-breathed and is therefore reliable in everything it says.

Are there historical errors in the Bible?

The answer is no, though men with a predisposition to discredit the Bible have rushed into print with lists of alleged errors, only to find that all they succeeded in discrediting were their own reputations for accuracy and objectivity.

Typical of the kinds of alleged historical errors of which the Bible is accused is its reference to one Tirhakah, king of Ethiopia. Scholars asserted that Tirhakah was only nine years of age and could not have been king of Ethiopia as the Bible says he was. Consequently, they cite the two passages in which he is named king of Ethiopia as examples of error in biblical history (cf. Isaiah 37:9; 2 Kings 19:9). Are they right? The answer is no. Edward J. Young, late professor of Old Testament at Westminster Theological Seminary, says, "It is certainly not the part of wisdom to declare that Scripture is here guilty of an error." He explains that Egyptian chronology of the period (which is the only other source of information) is uncertain. The entire period, he notes, is "fraught with difficulty." Hence, those who assert that the Bible is in error prove only that they wish to prove it is in error. The facts do not support the critics ("Are the Scriptures Inerant?" in *The Bible, The Living Word of Revelation,* Merrill C. Tenney, ed., pages 117, 118).

Many illustrations of this sort of thing could be given. Professor Young refers to a book purporting to give a list of so-called biblical errors, and he shows that the errors, so-called, are usually in the heads of the critics. For example, the Bible is said to claim that Shalmanezer captured Samaria in 722, when in fact it was Sargon. In support of this criticism of the Bible, the annals of Sargon's reign are quoted. Is there, in fact, a genuine mistake in Bible history?

Again, the answer is no. Professor Young makes the following points: first, the Bible does not actually say that Shalmanezer captured Samaria. Yet, he admits, it does imply as much (2 Kings 17:5, 6). Second, Samaria fell in 722 B.C., and Shalmanezer died not long afterward. He was succeeded by Sargon who, two years after the fall of Samaria, returned to Samaria and deported more of its inhabitants. The chronicles of Sargon's reign apparently refer to troubles in Samaria at a later date than the conquest attributed to Shalmanezer, in which case the biblical record cannot be called in question.

The point is, careful examination usually discloses a misreading of the texts of Scripture, or a determination to reject them in favor of sources apparently in conflict with the Bible, even when those sources may have no proven validity. In time archaeological discoveries usually attest the historical accuracy of the Bible. As Professor Young says, ". . . the Bible speaks with the voice of truth. . . . It has committed no historical blunder." We can trust our Bibles.

At this point it should be pointed out that there is a vast difference between errors and difficulties. Alleged errors usually turn out, on further study, to be only difficulties. And in many cases the difficulties have been solved, either by archaeological discoveries or by textual studies. The number of difficulties is small, and no real errors in the Bible have been confirmed. This is the testimony not only of Christians who wish to defend the authority of the Bible, but also of archaeologists who find themselves forced to do so. As a Yale university archaeologist says, "On the whole . . . archaeological work has unquestionably strengthened confidence in the reliability of the scriptural record. More than one archaeologist has found his respect for the Bible increased by the experience of excavation in Palestine" (Millar Burrows, *What Mean These Stones?*, page 1).

An inescapable conclusion is that refusal to believe the Bible usually stems from prejudice. The unbeliever is predisposed to reject the Bible, and no amount of evidence supporting its accuracy will make him change his mind. It's a pity, because there is no other source of information about God. And, as Jesus says, "There is a judge for the one who rejects me and does not accept my words; that very word which I spoke will condemn him at the last day. For . . . the Father who sent me commanded me what to say and how to say it. I know that his command is eternal life. So whatever I say is just what the Father has told me to say" (John 12:48-50).

Someday unbelievers will learn to their grief that the Book they scorned was indeed the Word of God, a message of eternal life. How sad to have rejected that!

What is meant by the "infallibility" of Scripture?

One of the fundamentals of Christian belief is the infallibility of Scripture. It could almost be said that this is the starting-point, this is *the* fundamental truth. In theory, other truths are more important. Take, for example, the truth of Christ's resurrection; without that, there is nothing. But without an infallible Bible, there is no reliable testimony about the resurrection, nor is there a reliable interpretation of its meaning. Thus, the infallibility of Scripture is crucial.

What does *infallibility* mean? Simply put, it means that the Scriptures cannot teach deception; there are not and cannot be mistakes in the Bible. The Bible itself teaches this, and Christians on every educational level have believed it since the first century. Augustine, one of the early theologians and church Fathers, said, "I believe most firmly that not one of those authors (of the Bible) has erred in any respect in writing." Luther said flatly that "the Scriptures have never erred," and John Wesley agreed. "If there be any mistakes in the Bible," he said, "there may well be a thousand. If there be one falsehood in that book, it did not come from the God of truth."

It should be understood that from the beginning, belief in the infallibility of Scripture was virtually unanimous, held by theologians of every branch of what may be termed the Christian church. Furthermore, it endured the vicissitudes of time, until fairly recently. Some theologians no longer believe in the possibility of a divine revelation. They do not believe that God is willing to make himself known in Scripture—which makes you wonder why they are theologians. Most of us would be unwilling to pursue studies about God unless we were convinced that something reliable could be discovered. But whatever the explanation of their unbelief may be, for all of us the important question about the Bible is, "Are there errors in it?"

The answer—which I personally assert with confidence—is no, there are no errors in the Bible. It is God's infallible Word. As Paul says—with reference to the Bible—"All Scripture is God-breathed" (2 Timothy 3:16), a statement which surely carries with it the idea of infallibility.

Paul is right, and those who say otherwise are wrong. Their position leaves them without a word from God. All they have to listen to is themselves, and their voices are the muttering of lost souls who don't know where they have come from or where they are going.

It doesn't take much thought to perceive the seriousness of these modern attacks on the infallibility of Scripture. Most of us who read and love the Bible believe that it is divinely inspired—which it is not if it is fallible. Who can believe that God makes mistakes? Thus, if the Bible has mistakes, it is not divinely inspired; it did not come from God. And if God is not its author, its teaching is not binding on Christians or anyone else; it is a book without authority. You are free to take it or leave it, as you wish.

There have always been those who thought they could find mistakes in the Bible. Others deny that there can be a written self-disclosure of God.

The trouble is, theologians who do this wreck theology. They spend their time speculating about this and that, and in the process create a theology of nonsense. Having cut themselves off from the objective truths revealed in Scripture, they are doomed to prattle meaningless things. As one believing theologian, Clark Pinnock, expresses it, "There is no valid stopping place between the possession of valid information about God and salvation, and the despairing realization of no revelation at all. The denial of objective and propositional revelation in Scripture is deeply nihilistic for theology. It dooms the venture at its outset."

No wonder churches are half-filled, or empty. Who wants to listen to a theologian speculate about things of which he has no more, and possibly less, certainty than the man in the pew? Not I, and not you. We prefer listening to the prophets who spoke with energy because they knew they had a word from the Lord. Or we listen to Jesus Christ, our Lord, who claimed that he said only what God the Father was saying; or we listen to the apostles who, like Paul, spoke with authority.

As Paul says—in so many places—"We know" and "I want you to know . . ." He knew the source of the Scriptures was the living God who spoke through the prophets and the apostles. His Word is truth, his Word is infallible. What this means is that we can trust our Bibles. Let the theologians play with their subjective perceptions of truth; we shall hold fast to the infallible, inerrant Word of God, the Bible.

The Bible's claim for itself is that Scripture contains divine truth, expressed in human language, free from error. Freedom from error is guaranteed by the inspiration of the Holy Spirit. He inspired not only the thoughts the writers expressed, but the very words.

If we did not know this to be true, we could have no assurance of salvation. But God's truthfulness is the basis of our assurance. As John writes, "We accept man's testimony, but God's testimony is greater because it is the testimony of God. . . ." John goes on to tell us something about the subject of God's testimony, which we have in the Bible. It is about his Son, Jesus Christ, our Lord. "This is the testimony," John says, "God has given us eternal life, and this life is in his Son. He who has the Son has life; he who does not have the Son of God does not have life" (1 John 5:9, 11).

There is an objective statement of truth from God. Do you believe it?

In the preface of some novels or other forms of fiction, there may be found a notice for the reader. It says something to the effect that the characters and incidents related are purely fictional; any similarity to real people or happenings is unintended and is accidental. The purpose of the notice to the reader is obvious; the author wishes the reader to know that he is reading a work of fiction, not a biography. The characters in the story are his own invention.

The Bible is different; it makes it quite clear that its characters are real, every incident happened exactly as related, and the telling is designed to make a point. In other words, the Bible is true, and it teaches truth. Not only so, but it claims for itself divine authorship—which means that God himself is its source. Thus, two ideas—at least— are immediately grasped: that the Bible is inspired, and it is infallible. It is infallible (meaning that it cannot teach deception) because God is its author. God can neither lie nor be deceived, and still be God.

That this is the Bible's testimony to its own character is clear from a number of passages. Here are a few: "All Scripture is God-breathed" (2 Timothy 3:16); the Scripture cannot pass away and cannot be broken (Matthew 5:19; John 10:35); its very words are taught by the Holy Spirit (1 Corinthians 2:13); when the prophets speak, it is God himself who speaks through them (Romans 9:25); men who were moved by the Holy Spirit spoke from God (2 Peter 1:21).

The Scriptures not only trace their source to God himself, but declare firmly that God cannot lie—and he insists that his servants must also speak the truth (Numbers 23:19; Matthew 19:18; Ephesians 4:25; Colossians 3:9). As Clark Pinnock says, "Divine truthfulness is the rock beneath biblical infallibility. . . . Infallibility is essential to the basic belief in Scripture as God's inspired Word." This point is made by the Apostle John in his warning that "anyone who does not believe God has made him out to be a liar, because he has not believed the testimony God has given about his Son" (1 John 5:10). The Scriptures contain error only if they are not inspired or

God is untrue. Neither idea is acceptable; neither squares with the facts before us as we examine our Bibles.

A point sometimes overlooked is that Jesus believed implicitly in the integrity of the Scriptures. He believed they were God's Word. If we believe in him as Savior and Lord, we must accept his view of Scripture. It is inconceivable that the Lord could have been mistaken; in fact, he said that his teaching was not his own (John 7:16). It was from God, including his view of the Scriptures. Thus, anyone who rejects Christ's teaching, including his teaching about the nature of the Scriptures, rejects God.

He also said that if anyone chooses to do God's will, he will find out whether his teaching came from God. And in that statement we may have the explanation we are seeking for widespread rejection of the Bible. Those who truly choose to do the will of God accept the Bible as his Word. Is the converse true also—that those who reject the Bible prove that they don't really want to do the will of God?

Infallibility and inerrancy of Scripture are related, inseparable ideas. A dictionary defines infallible as "that which makes, or is capable of making, no mistakes." An infallible authority is unfailingly true; its judgments and doctrines are *always* correct.

The dictionary defines inerrant as "that which contains no errors." Thus, to say that the Scriptures are inerrant is to claim for them absolute freedom from error of any kind. There are no mistakes, no errors in the Bible.

Many people find this hard to swallow. In their minds, it is asking too much to expect people to believe that a book written by human beings is totally free from error. You can understand their hesitation. Yet inerrancy is a logical conclusion, since an infallible book must be inerrant. If a book is incapable of making mistakes, its teaching must be free from mistakes. This conclusion is, in turn, dependent upon the idea of inspiration. If God inspired the writers, he inspired them to write what is true.

There are, of course, those who would like to find a compromise between the ideas of infallibility and inerrancy—a position in which mistakes are admitted while defending the truth of inspiration. The rub is, compromise here is an impossibility. Either the Bible is divinely inspired, in which case it is utterly reliable in all its parts, or it is not. If it is divinely inspired, it is true in all its parts, since God cannot lie.

Two alternative views are possible, but they lead to the same conclusion: a Bible that cannot be trusted. The first of the two views denies inspiration. According to this view, the Bible is just a collection of myths and nice stories. The second alternative view accepts inspiration, but says it applies to parts of the Bible, not to the book in its entirety. This sounds better than a rejection of inspiration, but it still leaves us with a book that cannot be trusted.

Why not trust a Bible that is, in theory, inspired yet not inerrant? The answer is obvious: if the writers of the Bible were capable of error in one particular, who is to say they were not mistaken in others? Furthermore, if they were capable of errors in *any* particular, how are we to determine *which* of their doctrines are true and which are false?

It's easy to see that only two logical positions are permissible: either the Bible is God's infallible, inerrant Word, or it is not.

As for me, I believe the Bible is God's Word—free from error and utterly reliable. I stake my soul on this. How about you?

Does the Bible have answers for life in the twentieth century?

Can a Book written before the space age have relevant answers for modern life? Yes—if we ask the right questions. There are, of course, people who ask no questions, or ask questions of trivial importance; for them the Bible has no answers. Having no serious questions, people of this nature rarely, if ever, open the covers of a Bible. Even so, many of them feel competent to pass judgment on the Bible. Folks who would admit without hesitation their incompetence to comment on any other book they have neither read nor studied often feel perfectly qualified to write off the Bible, notwithstanding their ignorance of its contents.

However, those who ask the right questions find answers in the Bible. The testimony not only of unnumbered millions of believers of past generations, but also in these times is that the answers the Bible gives are the right answers—relevant answers to crucial questions.

One important question every sensible person should ask himself is, Where did I come from, or who am I? The Bible says plainly that we were all made in the image of God. He is the source of our life and breath and in fact of every good thing we see on earth.

Another good question is, How should I live? "To act justly and to love mercy and to walk humbly with (my) God" (Micah 6:8)—this is what God "requires" of me. Requires? Yes, requires. It's important to know this.

Perhaps the most serious question is, Where will I spend eternity? Anybody can see that that is a serious question. But where can you find the answer except in the Bible? The Bible says that God has prepared a home for those who love him and trust him. The Bible speaks of the future in terms of eternal life. As Jesus said, "I tell you the truth, whoever hears my word, and believes him who sent me has eternal life and will not be condemned; he has crossed over from death to life" (John 5:24).

In my thinking, that's *the* best answer to *the* most important question anyone can ask. But if you don't think the Bible has the answer, perhaps you aren't asking the right questions.

Modern society is basically no different from any other society that has ever lived. Men are fundamentally unchanged, and their deepest needs are unchanged from what they have always been. Society even asks the same questions it has always asked (Where did we come from, and where are we going?).

No answers to those questions have ever been found except in the Bible. Or at least no *satisfactory* answers. I know scientism talks confidently about man's evolution up from the slime of some primeval swamp, but for me it's hard to take such theorizing seriously. Even if it could account for bones, blood, and sinews—which it can't—it would leave unanswered the truly significant questions about man's spiritual nature, such as his consciousness of God and his sense of sin and alienation.

Only the Bible can tell us where we came from, and only the Bible can shed any light whatsoever on the world beyond the grave. The Bible tells me I was made in the image of God; it also tells me that image is flawed by sin, and that God will judge me for that sin unless I can be forgiven and cleansed. The answer? Jesus Christ. He is the answer to the real problems all of us face. The Apostle Paul explained that "in him [i.e., in Christ] we have redemption through his blood, the forgiveness of sins . . ." (Ephesians 1:7). The words "in him" may puzzle some, but they aren't really mysterious; they describe those who simply believe the gospel and open their hearts to Jesus Christ. He immediately shares his own life with them, so that they can be described as "in him." "United to him" is a fair equivalent.

The Bible also tells us how to live meaningful lives. For us Christians, life is not a pointless existence; we don't just hang in there until we die. The Bible teaches us how to live as sons of God—i.e., those whose real life comes from him, who for that reason belong to him. The Bible tells us how to live meaningful lives, and for that reason alone it is relevant for these times. The truth is, it's the one truly relevant book in existence; it is in a class by itself, the living Word of God. And since it is the Word of God, asking whether the Bible is relevant is like asking whether we really need God.

Are all Bible teachers reliable?

There is scarcely a truth in the Bible that may not be distorted and has not in fact actually been distorted by someone in the long history of the church.

Take the truth that the Holy Spirit of God is the divine interpreter of God's Word. Has this truth been distorted? Yes, and it still is being wrested by those who discard the traditional teaching of the church, replacing it with ideas born in their own heads. They even claim the inspiration of the Holy Spirit for their ideas. Furthermore, they quote Scripture to prove it: ". . . you do not need anyone to teach you" (1 John 2:27). This, they contend, supports them in their rejection of traditional views and the assertion of their own.

The rub is, the line they quote is only part of a verse which, in turn, is only part of a paragraph which teaches just the opposite of what that short statement *seems* to teach. Here is the entire passage: "See that what you have heard from the beginning remains in you. If it does, you will also remain in the Son and in the Father. And this is what he promised us—even eternal life. I am writing these things to you about those who are trying to lead you astray. As for you, the anointing you received from him remains in you, and you do not need anyone to teach you. But as his anointing teaches you about all things and as that anointing is real, not counterfeit—just as it has taught you, remain in him" (1 John 2:24-27).

What is John saying? That the source of their knowledge of the truth was, first, the apostles themselves, and, second, the Holy Spirit of God who confirms in every true believer's mind the truth that the apostles taught. Elsewhere, what they taught is termed the apostles' doctrine or teaching (Acts 2:42). In still another place it is pointed out that the salvation which was at first announced by our Lord, was confirmed to the second generation of believers by those who heard him directly. God, in turn, validated their testimony by "signs, wonders, and various miracles, and gifts of the Holy Spirit" (Hebrews 2:3, 4).

The gifts of the Holy Spirit were (and still are) people endowed with what may be termed talents, abilities, or enablements. Among them are teachers—men enabled by the Holy Spirit of God to teach. But what they teach has already been defined; it is the faith that God has once for all entrusted to the saints (Jude 3). It is the apostles' doctrine, the teaching given them so long ago by the Holy Spirit, the divine author of the Scriptures.

Everything a man says in his capacity as a teacher of religious things should (indeed, *must*) be tested by the Scriptures. Only those whose teaching meets the plumb line test of the Scriptures can be trusted. All others may be safely ignored.

How can I effectively discover what the Bible is saying to me?

Some thoughts in the Bible are easily grasped, as in Genesis 1:1, "In the beginning God created the heavens and the earth." Others are more difficult to understand. Some verses require more diligent study; their meaning does not lie on the surface. This should not surprise us. After all, the Bible is not a comic book; it is a revelation of truth about the most profound matters imaginable.

Nevertheless, God does not intend to mystify us; the Bible is a revelation, not a puzzle, and God wants us to understand it. One reason why many do not understand the Bible is that they don't study it; they assume that it is too tough for them, thinking perhaps that only ministers or preachers are equipped to understand it. This is a serious mistake; from the beginning the Bible has been understandable to ordinary people who take the time to study it. After all, the apostles who wrote most of the New Testament were untrained men. This doesn't mean they were dumb or illiterate; it means only that they had no formal training in theology. They didn't know any big words, and didn't use any (cf. John 7:15; Acts 4:13).

Why did God use them as his spokesmen? He had at least two good reasons: first, he wanted to be understood by nonprofessional people. If he had given his message through philosophers and theologians, it might have come through garbled; at the very least, it would have been largely incomprehensible to most of us. Second, God has no use for human pretensions. We confer degrees on each other, but these mean nothing to God. He regards the wisdom of the world as sheer foolishness, and why not? The best brains in the world's history have never discovered anything meaningful about God or life after death. So God has chosen those whom the world's intellectuals regard as fools to shame the bright and the wise, as the world's intellectuals regard themselves.

These remarks should not be construed as contempt for education. Such is not the case. A good education is a great privilege, and it confers an advantage on its possessor. The idea here is that lack of it does not preclude a fine grasp of the Scriptures. All it takes to know and understand the Bible is a combination of three things: a right attitude, a personal relationship with God through our Lord Jesus Christ, and study.

The place to begin Bible study is an examination of your heart to determine what you really think about doing the will of God. This is where success or failure is decided, for if you do not really want to do the will of God, you will never succeed in understanding the Bible.

This point is well made in a conversation Christ had with a few religious leaders. They were amazed at the quality of his teaching; he taught with authority which they obviously envied. They were forever quoting their teachers and their teachers' teachers. Jesus, on the other hand, spoke as the authority himself and was somehow convincing.

Yet they did not want to be convinced. Why not? Because he had not been trained in their schools for rabbis, and he had no degrees. His success as a teacher seemed to minimize the importance of their education and their credentials as religious gurus. So they said, in effect, "since this man is not formally trained, what makes him think he is qualified to teach?" (cf. Mark 1:22; John 7:14ff.).

In reply, Jesus explained that his teaching was not innovative, it was not something he had thought about, not a personal system of his own. "My teaching is not my own," he said. "It comes from him who sent me" (John 7:16). What he meant was that what he teaches is divine truth. Though he became man, he never did or said anything independently of his Father in Heaven. Thus, what Jesus does is what God in Heaven does; what Jesus says is what God in Heaven says.

That was a bold claim. The rabbis regarded it as blasphemous, and on more than one occasion they tried to stone him to death (cf. John 10:33). But Jesus explained their problem: they did not really want to do the will of God. If they had, they'd have acknowledged that his teaching was from God. "If a man chooses to do God's will," Jesus said, "he will find out whether my teaching comes from God or whether I speak on my own" (John 7:17).

This is the crucial factor in success or failure in Bible study: willingness, even determination to do the will of God. In Christ's day many were unwilling to do the will of God; thus, they were rendered incapable of understanding the basics, such as the source of Christ's teaching.

If you do not make it your amibition to please God, forget about Bible study; you'll never understand it. The pity is, you may lose your soul.

A second essential for understanding the Bible is a personal relationship with God. Without it, you lack the help that God himself gives his children who seek to understand his Word.

The truth is that, unaided, none of us would understand much that is in the Bible, and we certainly would not be concerned about applying it to our lives. We need the help of the Holy Spirit, who sets up the personal relationship we are talking about, then helps us understand the Bible.

But how is such a personal relationship with God achieved? The answer is, it depends upon you, and it depends upon God. Your part comes first. On a holiday in Jerusalem Jesus stood in a public square and called out to the people, "If a man is thirsty, let him come to me and drink. Whoever believes in me, as the Scripture has said, streams of living water will flow from within him" (John 7:37, 38).

What did he mean? The Apostle John explains. "By this he meant the Spirit, whom those who believed in him were later to receive." Thus, the personal relationship with God about which we are talking is possible only when you (or I) respond to the gospel by coming to Christ. "Coming" means believing in him. He then does his part: he gives us the Holy Spirit of God. It is this action, of course, that truly establishes the relationship; when God's Spirit comes into our lives, we are born from above and become God's own children.

This means that we have eternal life. It also means that we have a divine helper who enables us to understand God's Word. This is the truth Paul had in mind when he wrote that "no one knows the thoughts of God except the Spirit of God. We have . . . received . . . the Spirit who is from God, that we may understand what God has freely given us" (1 Corinthians 2:11, 12).

In the same context Paul explains that non-Christians cannot understand the Bible. "The man without the Spirit," he says, "does not accept the things that come from the Spirit of God, for they are foolishness to him, and he cannot understand them, because they are spiritually discerned" (verse 14).

Thus, a personal relationship with God—which is established by God's own Spirit when we come to Christ, believing—is absolutely essential if we are to understand the Bible. If this is true—as it obviously is—what does this say about your inability to understand the Bible, or lack of desire to do so?

Sin is lawlessness. (1 John 3:4)

Just as he who called you is holy, so be holy in all you do; for it is written: "Be holy, because I am holy." (1 Peter 1:15, 16)

Anyone who does wrong will be repaid for his wrong. (Colossians 3:25)

Do not be deceived: God cannot be mocked. A man reaps what he sows. The one who sows to please his sinful nature, from that nature will reap destruction; the one who sows to please the Spirit, from the Spirit will reap eternal life. (Galatians 6:7, 8)

6/WHAT DOES THE BIBLE SAY ABOUT RIGHT AND WRONG?

We all face difficult moral choices every day. Some people even claim that anything goes. Are there standards of right and wrong, and how can we find out what they are?

How can we tell right from wrong?

God built into us a moral sense, so that we know instinctively that some things are wrong and others right. The Apostle Paul spoke of masses of people who, not having any written revelation of truth, nevertheless understood the difference between right and wrong. He said they show the work of the law written in their hearts (Romans 2:15). Their consciences told them when they were on the right track and when they were straying.

It should be understood that the conscience is not so much a faculty as it is the exercise of judgment with reference to moral truth. The Bible mentions certain persons whose consciences are dead, as if burnt with a hot iron (1 Timothy 4:2). These are genuinely psychopathic personalities, but the fault is theirs; in all likelihood they began by accommodating themselves to a consciousness of evil in their lives, and ended up incapable of exercising moral judgment. Their consciences are now dead.

The Bible also speaks of "defiled" and "corrupted" consciences, meaning that the persons in question are aware of evil in their lives and may even be distressed by it (see 1 Corinthians 8:7; Titus 1:15). Happy is the person whose conscience troubles him to the point where, confessing, he comes to Christ and is cleansed of his evil conscience (Hebrews 10:22).

It should be obvious that the conscience is a fallible guide. One Bible passage speaks of having the senses "trained . . . to distinguish good from evil" (Hebrews 5:14). This means that the conscience is only as reliable as it is made to be. It must be instructed, and the source of instruction is the Word of God. The Apostle Paul reminded his young friend Timothy that as a child he had learned the Scriptures which, Paul said, are "useful for teaching, rebuking, correcting and training in righteousness" (2 Timothy 3:16). So the final authority in matters of ethics, or any other aspect of the problem of discerning between good and evil, is the Bible. Not culture, not a people's preferences, not circumstances, but the Bible.

In ancient times many false prophets were making their pitch in Israel. The prophet of God, Isaiah, warned the people about the danger of listening to such false prophets. They were told to test every word they heard, and the standard of truth was the Scripture. The standard is the same today. We know right from wrong by listening to what God says in his Word, the Bible.

If everybody is doing it, is it okay?

Absolutely not! The proper standard whereby an action may be judged is not its popularity. The only valid standard is the Word of God. The crowd is often wrong. And if the crowd does something intrinsically wrong, that does not make it right; it means only that the crowd is wrong.

One of the lessons of history is that righteousness, decency, godliness—whatever you wish to call it—is usually pursued by a minority, not by the majority. The crowd takes the path of least resistance. But men of honor and character do what is right, even when the crowd is against them. The English poet Tennyson speaks somewhere of "civic manhood firm against the crowd."

The poet's lines echo Paul's words to Timothy. After describing the evil prevalent in his times, and noting that many—if not the majority—follow the path of folly, Paul says, "But as for you . . ." That is a recurrent line in Paul's final message to Timothy (2 Timothy 3:10, 14; 4:5). "As for you . . ." What it means is quite clear: the crowd may be doing many things, thinking that if so many people are doing the things in question, they must be all right. But as for you, don't imitate them; instead, continue in what you have learned, knowing that what you learned from your godly grandmother and from your godly mother and finally from me, Paul, is derived from Scripture and is therefore reliable. Take your instruction from the Scriptures; the sacred writings are able to equip you intellectually and in every other way for knowing right from wrong, for making proper choices, and in other ways living a useful life before the living God.

Paul obviously believed that the crowd would lead a man to perdition. He did not regard what the world may term *religion* as a mere option; it *is* an option, to be sure, but the alternative is damnation. Thus, for sensible people it is not an option worth considering. Futhermore, it is the living God who determines just what incurs his wrath and what is pleasing to him. Perhaps the crowd wouldn't judge you for, say, sexual immorality. In fact, in these times many regard infidelity with sublime nonchalance. But God will judge you; he even describes himself as the avenger of those who are sinned against in this respect.

So the answer to the question, "Is it right if everybody is doing it?" is, No. It is right only if God says so, and the only reliable source of information about his opinion in any matter is the Bible.

What do you think of the new morality?

It doesn't matter what I think about it; it's God's opinion that counts. *Opinion* is hardly the right word here, since God has no mere opinions, as if he also evaluated questions and came up with his own ideas. All his judgments are true. It was our Lord himself who said in his prayer to the Father, "Your word is truth." He said that for our sakes, because his prayer for us was that God would sanctify us in the truth. Well, what is truth? God's Word is truth. So the idea we get from this is that submission to the Word of God makes Christians different; it sets them apart.

This means that we will both loathe and fear the new morality. We fear it because we know the tendencies of our own hearts; it is so easy to give way to evil, especially when we know our neighbors will not condemn us for it. It's easy to lapse into a life-style that satisfies every natural desire without subjecting those desires to the disciplines or restraints imposed on them by the Word of God. So we fear the new morality—for ourselves and for those we love.

We also loathe it, because God loathes it. There are such strong statements about impurity in the Bible that no one can mistake their meaning. For example, Paul wrote that "it is God's will that you should be holy; that you should avoid sexual immorality" (1 Thessalonians 4:3). That's plain enough for anyone. It's significant that God calls himself the avenger of those who are sinned against sexually (see 1 Thessalonians 4:6; Hebrews 13:4; 1 Corinthians 6:9, 10). "God will judge the adulterer and all the sexually immoral" (Hebrews 13:4). Many "swingers" sin with an abandon nowadays, confident that their own liberated generation will not judge them or condemn them for their sexual license. Maybe not. But God will judge them. That's what the Bible says. Just what is meant by that is made plain in a passage like this: "Do you not know that the wicked will not inherit the kingdom of God? Do not be deceived: neither the sexually immoral nor idolaters nor adulterers nor male prostitutes nor homosexual offenders nor thieves nor the greedy nor drunkards nor slanderers will inherit the kingdom of God" (1 Corinthians 6:9, 10). That says it all. And if that's what God thinks about the "new morality," what should I think?

Is it ever right to tell a lie?

Convenient perhaps, but not right. I can't think of an occasion when it may be right to tell a lie. Now, I am assuming that our definition of a lie is the same as Mr. Webster's. According to the dictionary on my desk, a lie is "an assertion of something known or believed by the speaker to be untrue with intent to deceive." In other words, a lie is a false statement that is deliberately misleading.

It should be admitted that more than one honored figure in the Bible was caught in a deliberate lie. The Bible is the world's most realistic book; it portrays even its heroes as they were, warts and all. However, there is no hint of divine approval of lying. In fact, every statement in the Bible about communication insists upon the plain truth. When the Apostle Paul wrote his letters, he assured his readers that he was telling the truth. "I speak the truth in Christ," he wrote the Christians in Rome, "I am not lying, my conscience confirms it in the Holy Spirit" (9:1). He said the same thing to the Galatians. "Have I now become your enemy by telling you the truth?" Paul wrote (4:16).

There are ample warnings in the Bible about the consequences to be suffered by those who lie. Habitual liars, of course, are doomed (Revelation 22:15). Nobody who loves and practices lying will get into Heaven. As for Christians, lying is forbidden. God says, "Do not lie to each other . . ." (Colossians 3:9). The gist of the various biblical statements about telling the truth is that for those who love God and are subject to his Word, there is no alternative to the plain truth.

What about circumstances in which the truth could do unnecessary damage? Well, there's no commandment in the Bible to blurt out all the truth all the time. Withholding part of the truth is okay, provided: (1) there is no intent to deceive, and (2) withholding information does not *actually* deceive. I can think of occasions when it may not be wise to tell the whole truth. Take the case of a dying child, or an adult given to hysteria. In the case of the adult, the truth must be told eventually, but it might be better to prepare the person for it gradually. On at least one occasion our Lord withheld the truth from his brothers, refusing to tell them his plans. Check it for yourself in John 7. But he did not lie; he never lied. In fact, the Bible says it is impossible for God to lie (Hebrews 6:18).

It also says, however, that the Devil is a liar. Not only is he a liar, but he is the father of lies (John 8:44). That's something to think about the next time any of us feels tempted to tell a lie.

. . . God, the blessed and only Ruler, the King of kings and Lord of lords, who alone is immortal and who lives in unapproachable light, whom no one has seen or can see. To him be honor and might forever. Amen. (1 Timothy 6:15, 16)

The Lord is the everlasting God, the Creator of the ends of the earth. He will not grow tired or weary, and his understanding no one can fathom. (Isaiah 40:28)

For there is one God and one mediator between God and men, the man Christ Jesus. (1 Timothy 2:5)

No one has ever seen God, but God the only Son, who is at the Father's side, has made him known. (John 1:18)

7/WHAT SHOULD I REALLY THINK ABOUT GOD OR ABOUT JESUS CHRIST?

Everyone seems to have their own ideas about God, and they can't all be right. Since success in this life and in the life to come depends on God, it is important that we know what he is like.

Did man invent God?

One fairly common objection to belief in God is the notion that God is a figment of man's imagination. According to this view, man created God in his own image—not the reverse, as the Bible teaches. In support of this view, the skeptic points to the gods of the ancient Greeks and Romans. They were certainly very frail gods, sharing the vices as well as the virtues of the mortals who honored them—and their idiosyncracies too. They were just Greeks and Romans on a grand scale.

All this proves is that the gods of the Greeks and Romans were very much like Greeks and Romans. It does not prove that the Greeks and Romans invented the idea of God. The truth is, there is evidence in support of the assertion that Greek and Roman notions of God represent the deterioration of finer views once held. Polytheism is not the starting place from which a race gradually develops a monotheistic faith. The reverse is true.

This is the point Paul makes in his Epistle to the Romans. He says that from the beginning men knew God. However, they "neither glorified him nor gave thanks to him, their thinking became futile and their foolish hearts were darkened." Then what? Paul explains: "Although they claimed to be wise, they became fools and exchanged the glory of the immortal God for images made to look like mortal man and birds and animals and reptiles" (Romans 1:21-23).

This is the source of the polytheism of the ancient Greeks and Romans, and of other deities made in the image of man.

The God of the Bible, on the other hand, is not a product of human creativity. He is not the kind of God people invent. Instead, he is uncompromisingly holy and just, and he demands perfection in those who seek him. Long before Athens or Rome were founded, God set the standards for the ancient people of Israel. "Be holy, because I am holy," he said (Leviticus 11:44ff.; 19:2; 20:7; cited in 1 Peter 1:16). Later—much later—Jesus reaffirmed the standard: "Be perfect, therefore, as your heavenly Father is perfect" (Matthew 5:48).

This is an uncongenial standard; it does not allow us to do what we so often wish to do. No society has ever developed a standard like this, or conceived a God who demands it, yet is also loving and compassionate. The God of the Bible is not a human invention; he is the one true God who has revealed himself.

Those who reject him inevitably create gods of their own. They may be deities like the gods of the Greeks and Romans, or they may be something less tangible, yet nevertheless gods to be worshiped. For some moderns, money is a substitute for ancient deities. But even in ancient times there were those who honored money more than anything else. Jesus referred to this. "You cannot serve both God and Money," he said (Matthew 6:24). Thus, modern man isn't as smart as he likes to think. Too smart to believe in nymphs and fairies and gods that live on Mount Olympus, he serves ideals equally idolatrous.

Jesus' dictum still stands: those who worship God "must worship in spirit and in truth" (John 4:24). The truth about God is found in Scripture, and in Jesus himself. As he explains, "Anyone who has seen me has seen the Father"—that is, has seen God (John 14:9). If we want to know God, we know where to go. He exists, he has revealed himself to the world, and he is ready to reveal himself to all who come to him through Jesus Christ.

Do you believe this?

What is God like?

Sooner or later nearly every thoughtful person asks himself what God is like. Many answers have been given, but none of them really satisfies probing minds. Thoughtful people suspect that the gods the various races have worshiped are only products of their own minds. Men see themselves, analyze themselves, and extend their human qualities to figures who are grander than themselves and yet are basically the same.

The God about whom the Bible speaks (or, to be more accurate, the God who speaks to men through the Bible) is not the product of any man's mind; he is not an extension on a cosmic scale of human qualities. Just the opposite is true; men are made in his image. Everything we know about him we have learned from him by revelation, not by cogitation.

Has he told us what he is like? Yes, he has. The Bible gives us profound statements about God, such as these: "God is spirit" (John 4:24), meaning that he is not matter. In more than one place he is termed "the invisible God" (Colossians 1:15; 1 Timothy 1:17; 6:16; Hebrews 11:27). The Bible also says that "God is light; in him there is no darkness at all" (1 John 1:5). The Bible doesn't really explain this, but does apply it to our conduct. If we claim to have fellowship with God, yet walk in the darkness—i.e., live sinfully—we lie (1 John 1:6). It is surely significant that in another place the Bible says God is a "consuming fire" (Hebrews 12:29). Again, this is not so much a definition of God as an application of truth about him. The idea is that he will not put up with sin forever.

For us sinners, the most comforting statement about God is that he is love (1 John 4:8). The very next statement says that he showed his love by sending his one and only Son into the world that we might live through him. It's a great passage, telling us that God was not content with defining or describing himself. Instead, he incarnated himself. In the person of his Son he became man and in this way revealed himself to us.

So what is God like? A man named Philip asked Jesus that question, and Jesus' answer was, "Don't you know me, Philip? . . . Anyone who has seen me has seen the Father" (John 14:9; cf. verses 5-8). Paul expressed it theologically. Christ Jesus, he said, is "the image of the invisible God" (Colossians 1:15). So there's the answer to the question. God doesn't expect us to think of him in abstract terms, terms we cannot really grasp. He shows us what he is like in human form—in the person of Jesus Christ. And as far as we Christians are concerned, he is altogether lovely.

What does the universe tell us about God?

There are many evidences of order in the universe. Every scientist knows the universe is an orderly, predictable system; if it weren't predictable, there would be no science. But order in the universe raises an important question: is there purpose behind it?

Many scientists who are not Christians are willing to admit that there is mind or intelligence behind the order in the universe. With us, they also deny that the universe is the result of a biochemical accident. But we Christians go much further. We believe that God not only created the universe, but also manifested a special interest in the planet called Earth.

Scientists and philosophers who are willing to admit the possibility of purpose in the universe nevertheless scoff at the idea that this planet could be significant. We can understand their impatience with claims for the importance of the Earth. After all, it is only a medium-size planet in a relatively insignificant solar system. The sun itself is only one of perhaps a hundred thousand million other stars in a vast galaxy. Moreover, our galaxy is only one of thousands of millions of other galaxies scattered throughout the universe. The more we learn of the universe, the more physically insignificant the Earth becomes.

Yet this is where the action is, and it is this that makes the Earth important. As far as we can tell, there is no action in outer space—certainly not in our solar system. Spaceships landing on the moon and on Mars confirm our suspicions that these are empty, barren, burnt-out cinders. There is no sign of life. Consequently, even if they were a trillion times bigger than the Earth, they would be less important. The testimony of the Bible is that "the highest heavens belong to the Lord, but the earth he has given to man" (Psalm 115:16).

Hence, we Christians affirm the truth of purpose behind the order in the universe, and we say—because we believe the Bible teaches it—that God's purposes are centered in mankind. Included in God's purpose is the liberation of the creation itself from its bondage to decay (cf. Romans 8:21). The universe is running down, scientists say. This will stop when God's ultimate purpose for the heavens and the Earth is realized.

More vital to us is his purpose with respect to redemption. *This* is the theme of the Bible—the redemption of lost mankind through the incarnation and subsequent death, resurrection, and ascension of Christ. Paul speaks of God's "good pleasure, which he purposed in Christ, to be put into effect when the times will have reached their fulfillment—to bring all things in heaven and on earth together under one head, even Christ" (Ephesians 1:9, 10).

Scientists and others may not know it, but this is the lesson to be learned in the order in the universe. Behind the order stands the living God, Maker of Heaven and Earth, and the Redeemer of sinful mankind.

For us Christians, the only reasonable explanation for the existence of the universe to begin with is found in Genesis 1:1—"In the beginning God created the heavens and the earth." What this means is that God created the universe out of nothing. Nothing existed until he, by infinite power, called it into existence. He did not merely rework existing materials; he created the materials out of nothing. This is what the Bible plainly teaches—". . . what is seen was not made out of what was visible" (Hebrews 11:3). The Bible also says that God the Son was the Creator. "By him all things were created: things in heaven and on earth, visible and invisible, whether thrones or powers or rulers or authorities; all things were created by him and for him" (Col. 1:16; cf. John 1:3).

To accept this explanation requires faith. The Bible does not deny this fact. In fact, the Bible says that "by faith we understand that the universe was formed at God's command" (Hebrews 11:3). What this means is that the universe is unexplainable apart from faith. Every possible explanation begins with faith in something, including the explanations of those who would like us to think they are dispassionate scientists. For example, the "big bang" theorists assume as an act of faith that gases were "out there" waiting to explode. And they exercise enormous faith in believing that exploding gases would eventually evolve into green grass, brown cows, and people like you and me who think and wonder where we came from.

For us Christians it is much easier—and it makes considerably more sense—to believe that in the beginning God created the heavens and the earth. In fact, this is—to us, at least—the only sensible explanation available.

Is God good?

Is God good, and does he show his goodness in tangible ways? Yes, God is good. With reference to essential goodness, Jesus said, "There is only One who is good" (Matthew 19:17). His words echo those of the prophets who, like Jeremiah, said simply that "the Lord is good" (Jeremiah 33:11; Nahum 1:7).

Does God do good things? This is the clear testimony of the Old and New Testaments. Significantly, God's goodness and his loving-kindness are closely related. In response to Moses' prayer for a glimpse of his glory, God promised to make all his goodness pass before Moses. And in fulfillment of the promise to reveal his goodness, God proclaimed in Moses' hearing that he, the Lord, is "compassionate and gracious . . . slow to anger, abounding in love and faithfulness" (Exodus 33:19; 34:6). God is good, and his goodness expresses itself in compassion and loving-kindness.

In the centuries that followed that great proclamation, God proved that he meant what he said. After the dedication of Solomon's Temple, the people returned to their homes "joyful and glad in heart for all the good the Lord had done for his servant David and his people Israel" (1 Kings 8:66).

In the New Testament, goodness is the fruit of the Holy Spirit (Galatians 5:22). Or, as Paul also says, "The fruit of the light consists in all goodness, righteousness and truth" (Ephesians 5:9; cf. Romans 15:14). God reproduces in those who know him the desire to be good and to do good. As in the Old Testament, in the New Testament the connection between goodness and kindness is unmistakable.

Creation itself gives evidence of God's goodness. As someone has pointed out, "The sportive movement of animals, the cheerful song of birds, the varied hues and fragrance of flowers . . . the pleasure attached to intellectual and even bodily exertion, all testify to the beneficence of the Creator" (E. A. Litton, *Introduction to Dogmatic*

Theology, page 69). The creation was affected by sin, to be sure, and it sometimes seems to be out of control and therefore destructive. Nevertheless, even in its fallen state the creation manifests the goodness of God. As Litton also wrote, "If God had been indifferent to our happiness, he might have made, or permitted a rival Power to make 'everything we tasted bitter, everything we saw loathsome, everything we touched a sting, every smell a stench, and every sound a discord.' "

Yet he didn't make the world that way. He is good, and he is loving, and he implants in those who know him the holy desire to be like him. The earth is filled with his goodness.

Does God love some people more than others?

One of the Apostle Paul's greatest achievements was the recovery of a long-forgotten truth with two sides to it—"There is no difference between Jew and Gentile—the same Lord is Lord of all and richly blesses all who call on him" (Romans 10:12). There is no partiality, no favoritism with God. Paul's kinsmen knew there was only one God, but they seemed to be emotionally incapable of believing that he could be nice to Gentiles.

In the cultural capital of the pagan world, Athens, Paul made a profound statement about the nature of God. God, he said, "made the world and everything in it (and) is the Lord of heaven and earth and does not live in temples built by hands" (Acts 17:24). Paul explained that God himself "gives all men life and breath and everything else. . . . He made every nation of men . . . and he determined the times set for them and the exact places where they should live." For Paul's listeners (pagan Gentiles) it must have been mind-expanding to hear for the first time that there is only one God, who is God over the whole earth.

But Paul's Jewish friends made an opposite error. They thought they had a monopoly on God's mercy. Paul tried to straighten them out—with little if any success. What he did was quote their prophets and draw reasonable inferences from them. Take the prophet Joel. He said (with reference to cataclysmic events of the future) that "Everyone who calls on the name of the Lord will be saved" (Joel

2:32; quoted in Romans 10:13). In Paul's mind, that was a statement about God—not about people. If everyone who calls on him will be saved, then the same Lord is Lord of all, and he richly blesses all who call on him.

Certain fanatical Jews of the times might have argued that Joel was thinking only of Jews in Jerusalem. Maybe so, Paul would have replied. But there were dimensions to the prophecy that the Holy Spirit did not emphasize until Paul's day. Yet the truth was there—visible to as many as had their spiritual eyes open to see. Paul quoted another prophet, Hosea, to underline that point. Through that prophet God had spoken in the eighth century B.C. Here's what he said: "I will call them 'my people' who are not my people; and I will call her 'my loved one' who is not my loved one" (Hosea 2:23; quoted in Romans 9:25).

What did Hosea mean? Favors bestowed on Israel alone? Maybe that's all he had in his mind; maybe that was how he personally understood the utterance. But Paul knew better. Through the prophet God was telling the world that his mercy is not restricted to any single race or people. Jews or Gentiles—or any other classification that may be devised—all alike may receive mercy from the same Lord, who richly blesses *all* who call on him.

That's something to think about, but of what use is it unless you actually call upon the Lord?

If God loves everyone and Christ died for all, are all saved?

In Jesus' conversation with Nicodemus (John 3), the Savior affirmed the universality of God's love but repudiated universalism. He said that God loves the entire world; his love is universal, extending to all without exception. Universalism, on the other hand, is the belief that all will be saved eventually—a notion which receives no support in Scripture. In fact, Jesus clearly distinguished between the perishing and those who escape. He contrasted the doomed with those who find eternal life.

Universalism is an attractive idea. The thought that some men and women will spend eternity in Hell is very dreadful, and God himself weeps over the doom of those who refuse to be saved. When Jesus contemplated what lay before unbelieving Jerusalem, he wept. How much more dreadful is eternal doom than the destruction of an earthly city!

Nevertheless, universalism is an impossible doctrine for several reasons, only two of which need be mentioned here. First, it does violence to the biblical concept of God's righteousness. This is the point Paul makes when he tries to comfort certain believers then suffering persecution. "God is just; he will pay back trouble to those who trouble you," Paul writes. He goes on to say that God will deal out retribution "to those who do not know God and do not obey the gospel of our Lord Jesus. They will be punished with everlasting destruction and shut out from the presence of the Lord and from the majesty of his power . . ." (2 Thessalonians 1:6, 8, 9).

This is the concept that underlies the call for vengeance present in so many of the Psalms. "O Lord, the God who avenges, O God who avenges, shine forth!" is the opening line in the 94th Psalm. In this, as in every other case, it is an appeal for a vindication of God's righteousness as the Judge who will not tolerate evil. Universalism ignores this element in God's character.

Jesus repudiated universalism by distinguishing between the lost and the saved. No such distinction is possible if all men everywhere are eventually saved. Jesus said that whoever believes in him will not perish (John 3:16, 17). Thus, he does more than set the terms for salvation; he implies that the unbelieving are doomed. They perish.

Paul may have had this passage in mind when he made a similar distinction between the lost and the saved. In his letter to the Corinthians he says, ". . . the message of the cross is foolishness to those who are perishing, but to us who are being saved it is the power of God" (1 Corinthians 1:18). Certainly Paul was not a universalist.

This is not a purely academic discussion. If you have not been saved, you are lost. Until you come repenting, and in faith receive Christ into your heart and life, you will remain lost. And if you die lost, you will be eternally lost—than which no prospect could be more dreadful.

Universalism no, but universal love yes. "God so loved the world that he gave his one and only Son, that whoever believes in him shall not perish but have eternal life" (John 3:16). Since he loves you and provided for your salvation, you have no excuse for remaining lost. If you go on perishing, it is because you refuse to be saved. What more can God do than he has done? If you spend eternity in outer darkness, whose fault will it be?

Paul's great statement that "The same Lord is Lord of all and richly blesses all who call on him" (Romans 10:12) says a lot about God. But it also implies a human responsibility. The Lord is waiting and ready to bless, but not everybody gets the blessing. Only those who actually call to him are blessed. All others lose out—forever. And those who are permanently lost have only themselves to blame, for it was never God's will that they should be condemned. He richly blesses all who call on him.

Now that statement implies an ability on man's part to call in such a way that God will hear and answer. If not, Paul's claim is meaningless. That he intended his readers to believe that they could call and that God would respond is plain from other passages in the New Testament, in particular Paul's own writings. It is significant that in his speech to educated pagans in Athens, in which he discoursed on the nature of God, Paul said that certain acts of God were done deliberately in order that "men would seek him and perhaps reach out for him and find him" (Acts 17:27).

The rub is, nobody really seeks him or stretches out his hands to God. Not without help. Paul himself painted a very dark picture of the human race. "There is no one who understands," he said, "no one who searches for God" (Romans 3:11). Then is Paul's great statement about a God who richly blesses all who call to him ultimately meaningless—just theological double-speak?

The answer, of course, is no. When men refuse to seek the Lord, he seeks them. Adam sinned and hid himself among the trees of the Garden of Eden. God came looking for him. "Adam!" he called, "Adam, where are you?" God has never stopped searching for lost souls. He sent his Spirit into the world to convict the world of sin. Who else can make the human heart tender and turn it to God? Who else can persuade a hardened sinner to repent and believe the gospel (Acts 17:30)?

God expects sinners to respond to the pleading of the Holy Spirit, who probes consciences through the preaching of the gospel. He knows, of course, that not everyone will respond. In Ephesus Paul warned both Jews and Greeks publicly and from house to house that they must turn to God in repentance and have faith in the Lord Jesus Christ (Acts 20:21). He begged them to do so, on Christ's behalf (2 Corinthians 5:20). Paul said on one occasion that when he preached, it was as if "God were making his appeal through (him)." Yet not everybody believed. Not then, and not now.

The same was true in Isaiah's day. "Lord," he moaned, "who has believed our message?" And that same prophet expressed God's personal grief at the lack of response to his invitation. "All day long I have held out my hands to an obstinate people," God said (Isaiah 65:2; cited in Romans 10:21).

God calls, but not everybody responds. And if they lose their soul, whose fault is it?

Since God is infinite, is he beyond time?

God is indeed infinite—that is, without limitations of any kind. What does this mean? It means, among other things, that God had no beginning. You and I did. On a certain day in history we were born. Before that, we had no existence, except of course as a fetus in our mother's womb. God had no beginning; he has always existed, and this is the testimony of Scripture. In Psalm 90 Moses praises God because "Before the mountains were born, or you brought forth the earth and the world, from everlasting to everlasting you are God" (verse 2). For such a God, time is not reckoned as we reckon it— measured out in minutes, hours, days, and years. In his sight "a thousand years . . . are like a day that has just gone by, or like a watch in the night" (verse 4).

This is an important truth. The concept of eternity depends upon its validity, since only a God who had no beginning can have no ending. Only he can provide an eternity of bliss for those whom he blesses. The apostles were conscious of this, and in their doxologies they ascribe honor and eternal dominion unto him (cf. 1 Timothy 6:16; 2 Timothy 4:18). He is the eternal God (Romans 16:26).

This doesn't mean that God is not conscious of time, a cosmic dreamer for whom all the yesterdays and tomorrows flow together in timeless, undivided sequence. God is not bound by time; it does not measure his duration. Nevertheless, he is conscious of it. In fact, his purposes are developed according to what may be termed a divine calendar. This is evident from the first pages in the Bible. Abraham was promised a progeny and a land, but he was warned that 400 years would pass before his descendants took possession of the promised land (cf. Genesis 15:12ff.).

The Advent of our Lord was according to God's calendar. As Paul says, "when the time had fully come, God sent his Son, born of a woman, born under law, to redeem those under law, that we might receive the full rights as sons" (Galatians 4:4, 5). Did you catch that expression, "when the time had fully come"? The birth of Christ was no accident; it was planned and timed.

Later, when Christ began to preach, he announced that the time had come. "The time has come. The kingdom of God is near," he proclaimed (Mark 1:15). At the Ascension, his followers asked him if it was time for the Father to restore an earthly kingdom to Israel. Jesus told them it was not for them to know "the times or dates the Father has set by his own authority" (Acts 1:7). The point is, God is still working according to his timetable. We don't know when Christ will return, but we know two things: he will return, and the time for it was fixed long ago by the Father who sent him to Bethlehem "when the time had fully come." God is not bound by time; he is the eternal Father. But he works according to schedule.

For us, all that really matters is that "now is the time of God's favor; now is the day of salvation" (2 Corinthians 6:2). I pray that you will open your heart to the eternal God who offers you an eternal home, through faith in the Lord Jesus Christ.

What evidence shows that God is a personal being?

What do we mean when we speak of God as personal? The dictionary defines the term as meaning "rational and self-conscious; as, a *personal* God." What this means is that God is not a force, nor is he—as pantheists would have us believe—identifiable with nature. He is not the sun, moon, or stars, nor is he the fluttering of a leaf or the leaf itself. He is a person. He thinks, he feels, he wills.

Does God think precisely the same way we think? Probably not. He does not grope his way by trial and error to a logical conclusion. No doubt reference in the Bible to God's thoughts is somewhat misleading, but only because of our intellectual limitations. Unless

God describes himself in human terms, we are incapable of grasping even elementary truths about his nature. Hence, he speaks of himself as thinking and planning. A familiar passage is Isaiah 55:8, in which God is recorded as saying to ancient Israel, "My thoughts are not your thoughts . . ." The same Hebrew word is translated "plans" in various other passages. For example, in Jeremiah 29:11 the Lord says, "I know the plans I have for you" (cf. Jeremiah 18:8; Zechariah 1:6; 8:14). The idea is quite clear: God thinks, he plans.

Moreover, he knows what we think. The Bible is full of references to God's knowing. Satan himself was the first to admit it, though he distorted the truth and thereby succeeded in corrupting Eve. When Abimelech, king of Gerar, took Abraham's wife Sarah into his harem, God stopped him from touching her, and in a dream he appeared to the king and explained why. "I know you did this with a clear conscience," God said. God knew the man's motives, and for this reason had mercy on him (Genesis 20:6; cf. 22:12).

God's knowing is not always as reassuring as it was to Abimelech. Our Lord told certain members of the religious establishment of his times that though they were adept at justifying themselves before men, they couldn't do it before God. Why not? Because "God knows your hearts. What is highly valued among men is detestable in God's sight" (Luke 16:15).

Consequently, one should not be casual about the truth that God is personal. It is not a purely academic notion. The personal God of whom we speak not only knows what we think, but also measures our thoughts according to his thoughts and judges us accordingly. In the day of judgment of the lost, their thoughts will serve only as witnesses against them (cf. Romans 2:15, 16).

God not only thinks, but he also *feels;* and his feelings are described in terms that we mortals can understand. For example, the Old Testament has a number of references to God's anger. The first is in the book of Exodus, where it says that "the Lord's anger burned against Moses" when Moses resisted the will of God for him (4:14). The Old Testament also speaks of God's wrath (KJV), which is generally taken to be a stronger word than anger (cf. Deuteronomy 9:7; Genesis 49:7). As used in some Bible translations, "wrath" may express God's fixed attitude toward that which provokes him, and his determination to do something about it. Anger is his feeling.

Is this merely an anthropomorphism—that is, the ascribing of human attributes to God? No, it is not. When Christ was on earth he sometimes became angry. For example, before healing a man with a withered hand, he asked his opponents what they thought the law said with respect to healing on the Sabbath. They refused to answer, and he, knowing why they refused, was angry (Mark 3:1-6).

Consider in this connection Jesus' conversation with his disciples in the upper room. When Philip said, "Lord, show us the Father," Jesus told him in effect that seeing him (Jesus), Philip was looking at the Father (John 14:8, 9). The inescapable conclusion is that if Jesus in the flesh got angry, so does the Father in Heaven. He is not a coldly clinical thinking machine; he *feels*.

Anger and wrath are emotional accompaniments of God's holiness. He is also love, and he *feels* loving. His love is more than an attitude of goodwill toward man; it is the expression of a great divine heart throbbing with tenderness and compassion. The prophets proclaimed the tenderness of God's love for ancient Israel, none more beautifully than Hosea, "the prophet of the broken heart." "What can I do with you, Ephraim? What can I do with you, Judah?" God asks, as if in grief (6:4). "How can I give you up, Ephraim? How can I hand you over, Israel? . . . My heart is changed within me, all my compassion is aroused" (11:8).

Or take Malachi, who tells how the Lord grieves because his love for Israel gets only lip-service in response. "A son honors his father, and a servant his master," the Lord says. "If I am a father, where is the honor due me? If I am a master, where is the respect due me?" (Malachi 1:6).

Are these also only anthropomorphisms? Perhaps. But Christ loved his friends with great feeling. At the tomb of Lazarus he wept. Why? Because his friend had died? No, not that; he knew that he was going to raise Lazarus from the dead. He wept because his friends were brokenhearted. His love was warm and easily moved (John 11:33-35). In the Garden of Gethsemane he shook the disciples awake when they slept, needing their companionship (Mark 14:32ff.). Their weakness troubled him. And so did Judas' treachery. When Judas identified Christ by saying hello and planting a kiss on his cheek, the Lord said, "Friend, do what you came for" (Matthew 26:50). The heartbreak of a betrayed man is heard in that word, "friend."

The personal God with whom we have to do feels. Our own feelings are but a reflection of the image of God in us. But whereas ours are flawed by sin, his are perfect. When he is angry, he is always angry for the right reason. His love is consistent with his holiness. He loves and feels love perfectly. How good it is to be loved by him, and to know it!

Further evidence of God's being a person is this: he wills things; and he reveals his will to his creatures.

What do we mean when we say God wills things? We mean that what God plans, he is able to accomplish. The best laid schemes of mice and men go awry. Not so with God's plans. There is no power and there are no circumstances capable of frustrating him. What he intends to accomplish, he accomplishes.

> Remember this, fix it in mind, take it to heart, you rebels. Remember the former things of long ago; I am God, and there is no other; I am God, and there is none like me. I make known the end from the beginning, from ancient times, what is still to come. I say: My purpose will stand, And I will do all that I please. . . . What I have said, that I will bring about; what I have planned, that will I do. (Isaiah 46:8-11; cf. 14:24)

The New Testament confirms the testimony of Isaiah and the other prophets. Take Paul's Epistle to the Ephesians. In the first chapter he says we believers have been "predestined according to the plan of him who works everything in conformity with the purpose of his will." What does Paul mean? He says—among other things—that God has planned our future, and what he has planned for us will be accomplished. His will is supreme; no one or no agency can defeat the purposes of Almighty God.

Furthermore, the God who plans our future loves us. If it were not so, we should be most miserable creatures. He loves us without having perceived anything in us that should have drawn his love. He loves us simply because he is love. And Paul says that nothing can separate us from that love—"Neither death nor life, neither angels nor demons, neither the present nor the future, nor any powers, neither height nor depth, nor anything else in all creation, will be able to separate us from the love of God that is in Christ Jesus our Lord" (Romans 8:38, 39).

Why not? Because his love is perfect, unchanging. Who can overpower him and force him to change his plans? No one! He works all things according to the counsel of his will.

This isn't the whole story, of course. There are some things God cannot do. He cannot lie, he cannot deny himself, and he cannot (or will not) force an unbeliever to believe. Every permanently lost soul is a testimony to the defeat of God's purpose for that individual, for God is not willing that any one should perish. Those who perish have only themselves to blame. Like the ancient Pharisees, they too reject God's purpose for themselves (cf. Luke 7:30), and they suffer the consequences. God forbid that you should reject his purpose for you in salvation! Open your heart to the Savior. Trust him to forgive you and save your soul. If you do, nothing will ever be able to separate you from the love of God.

We also see God's personality in that he communicates with his creatures. In some respects, this is the most exciting aspect of his nature. One can conceive of Deity thinking and feeling, and even having purposes, yet handle the concept as a concept, nothing more. But a God who communicates with his creatures is a God to be reckoned with; he demands response on our part. And the response he wants is partnership in a relationship. He wants to be our Savior and Father-God, and he wants us to be his children. How does he communicate with us? He speaks to us through nature, in his Word, and in his Son, Jesus Christ.

The Apostle John says, "To all who received him (Jesus) . . . he gave the right to become children of God" (John 1:12).

Is the relationship real? Absolutely! As John explains, all "those who believed in his name," receiving him, are born of God. Thus, the God who communicates *truth* also communicates *life*. Could any God be more personal than this? He thinks, he feels, he plans, he accomplishes his plans, and he communicates with us. He tells us the truth; and if we believe him, he gives us eternal life in association with his beloved Son, Jesus Christ. No wonder the prophets sometimes exclaimed in amazement, "Who is a God like you?" (Micah 7:18).

How does God communicate with people today?

To answer the question, I'd like to quote a few texts from the Bible. The first says that in the past "God gave . . . many different glimpses of truth in the words of the prophets. . . . (He) has now, at the end of the present age, given us the truth in the Son" (Hebrews

1:1, *Phillips*). This tremendous statement says that now, in these times in which we live, God speaks to us in and through Jesus Christ.

The second great text is a personal testimony of the Apostle Paul. He said, "Christ did not send me to baptize, but to preach the gospel" (1 Corinthians 1:17). In the paragraph that follows, Paul emphasized both his preaching and its content—what he called "the message of the cross," and "Christ crucified." So we have two great ideas so far: first, that God speaks to us in the person of his Son, Jesus Christ, and second that God sends men to preach Christ. That doesn't mean to preach *at* Christ; it doesn't even mean to preach *about* him, not, at least, in the way we talk about various great personages. To preach Christ means to present him, to lift him up for observers to see and hear. And the central truth about him is his death—i.e., his crucifixion.

The only authentic information about Christ is found in the Bible, God's Word. Consequently, various texts emphasize the importance of that Word. The Apostle Peter told where it came from. "Men spoke from God as they were carried along by the Holy Spirit," he said (2 Peter 1:21). He also said that the Word of the Lord abides forever; it is Scripture (i.e., the words of God), which he gave us through men inspired by his own Holy Spirit of truth (see 1 Peter 1:25; 2 Peter 3:16).

One more text will suffice to make the point: Paul wrote that "all Scripture is God-breathed and is useful for teaching, rebuking, correcting and training in righteousness, so that the man of God may be thoroughly equipped for every good work" (2 Timothy 3:16, 17).

The conclusion to all this is that God communicates truth through the Bible. If you want to hear God's Word, read the Bible. And if anyone says his message is from God, test it by the Bible. There's nothing more pathetic than the victim of a religious charlatan. But there's no need to be duped. Examine everything carefully, Paul urged his readers. In other words, don't be gullible. Let God get through to you with his Word. "Test everything. Hold on to the good" (1 Thessalonians 5:21).

The Bible is sometimes called special revelation, a term which embraces two ideas: miraculous events, and divine words. Neither stands alone; together they testify to the character and purposes of God. Take the Exodus of Israel from Egypt as an example. Unlike subsequent mass migrations, the Exodus was attended by supernatural phenomena. The waters of an immense lake rolled back to permit the people to cross on dry land, but when the pursuing armies of the Egyptians tried to follow they were drowned. A thick cloud provided cover for Israel during the daytime, and at night a supernatural light guided their way. This all was—in the jargon of some theologians—a "salvation event."

Yet it would have been misunderstood and no doubt forgotten by subsequent generations if God had not given the event its correct interpretation. This he did through his spokesmen. After the death of Moses, Joshua reminded the people that it was the Lord acting on their behalf that had brought them out of bondage. The whole nation responded, "It was the Lord our God himself who brought us and our forefathers up out of Egypt, from that land of slavery, and performed those great signs before our eyes" (Joshua 24:17).

This is an example of a prophetic interpretation of an event. The Bible is full of them. Indeed, this is what the Bible is: a record of events and interpretations of them. Without the interpretations we would have no way of knowing that God—assuming that he was in some way involved in the event—is loving and merciful. We might conclude only that he is clever and capable, perhaps even capricious.

The prophets and the apostles tell us what the events mean. Unaided, they could not have done so. But the Holy Spirit of God revealed the truth to them, and they in turn to us. A fine example of event and interpretation revealing God's mercy and, of course, his love and concern for mankind is found near the end of John's Gospel. Reviewing the miracles he had talked about, John said "These are written that you may believe that Jesus is the Christ, the Son of God, and that by believing you may have life in his name" (John 20:31). That was John's inspired interpretation of the miracles Jesus did. His words interpret God's acts. In this way, God reveals himself to us, and we see that he loves us and wants to save us.

Who is Jesus?

Before his conversion Saul of Tarsus hated Christians and, as he explained many years later, was convinced he "ought to do all that was possible to oppose the name of Jesus of Nazareth" (Acts 26:9). And that is just what he did—all that was possible, even forcing Christians to blaspheme the name they adored. Then Saul became a Christian, and for the rest of his life he bowed the knee at the name of Jesus.

This happened because he discovered Jesus' true identity. On the road to Damascus Saul was struck down by a bright shining light. It was as if he had been hit by a bolt of lightning, except that it did not stun him. Though temporarily blinded, he was fully conscious. He heard a voice speaking to him, and knew it was divine. "Who are you, Lord?" he asked. The answer shocked him more than the sudden flashing of light. "I am Jesus," the voice replied, and Saul realized immediately that Jesus, whose followers he had been hounding to death, was who they said he was—the Messiah, the Christ of God. That great discovery changed his life.

For the rest of his life Paul—as he was known—preached everywhere that Jesus is Lord. For him it was the central truth of the universe, and the great fact of revelation. Paul began to understand the Hebrew Bible as he had never understood it before. This is clear from his use of it in his writings, as illustrated in a great passage in Romans 10. Paul wanted to make the point that God is impartial; he saves Gentiles and Jews alike on the same basis. And to prove his point Paul quoted from the Hebrew Bible—i.e., the Old Testament—giving it an interpretation that would never have occurred to him before that experience on the road to Damascus.

He quoted from the prophet Joel, who said: "Everyone who calls on the name of the Lord will be saved." Joel was talking about Jehovah, the God of Israel. But when Paul lifted that text from Joel's prophecy, he used it with reference to Jesus of Nazareth. "Everyone who calls on the name of the Lord Jesus will be saved." That's what Paul intended to say. That this is indeed the case is plain from a study of the entire paragraph. Paul argued that nobody could call on him unless they had heard of him. Faith, he explained, comes from hearing the message, and the message is heard through the word of Christ (verse 16). So Paul referred that great statement from Joel to Jesus Christ.

What this means is that Jesus is God. Paul regarded him as truly and in all respects Deity. This is why he was confident that Jesus is a mighty Savior. Only God can save men's souls, and Jesus is God. As Paul wrote elsewhere in the same Letter to Romans, "Christ . . . is God over all, forever praised!" (Romans 9:5).

No wonder Paul bowed before him. The wonder is that so many refuse to do so. How about you?

What does Jesus Christ, who was born almost 2,000 years ago, have to do with us today?

The nineteenth-century historian and skeptic Ernest Renan (1823-1892) admitted that "the whole of history is incomprehensible without the Christ" (*La Vie de Jesus,* 1863). Yet Renan wrote only as a historian; he felt no personal need of Christ, no sense of him as a living being. The testimony of the Bible is that "Jesus Christ is the same yesterday and today and forever" (Hebrews 13:8). If so, the claims he made in Palestine nearly 2,000 years ago are as urgent as when he first made them.

What does Jesus Christ have to do with us who are living in the twentieth century?

Everything or nothing—depending on our personal response to what the Bible says about him. The very first page of the New Testament makes stupendous claims on his behalf. His name was given supernaturally, in advance, to tell *what* he was. *Jesus* means "Savior." Another name tells *who* he was. *Immanuel* means "God with us." Do you believe that Jesus was indeed God—God that became a man? And do you believe that he came to save you from your sins? If you do, he will mean *everything* to you—even as he did to Joseph and Mary, and the shepherds and the wise men, and thousands of others who have worshiped him.

Not everyone believed in him, to be sure. In fact, Jerusalem was upset when news of his birth reached the city. King Herod tried to kill him, but killed every baby except the one he was after in Bethlehem and its suburbs. That was not the last attempt on Christ's life; there were many others, and eventually, when he decided that the time had come, they succeeded in killing him.

They thought they had gotten rid of him. But they hadn't, of course. He rose from the dead and showed his wounded hands and side to his friends. They then scattered around the populated world and told others about him. Those who believed the message called him Lord. "Jesus is Lord!"—that was their confession of faith. Those who believe the message nowadays make the same confession: Jesus is Lord. Obviously, to those who make this confession Jesus Christ means everything—just as much as he meant to his original disciples. After all, if he was God then, he is God now.

Many people say he means nothing to them; they don't believe in him. The rub is that he will be every man's judge. This is the plain teaching of the Bible. So, while everybody has two options—to believe in him or to reject him—nobody can really say Jesus is nothing to me. He is either your Savior and Lord, or he will be your judge. You may choose, but choose you must, and "now is the time of God's favor, now is the day of salvation" (2 Corinthians 6:2) for as many as wish to obey the gospel and receive Jesus into their hearts and lives. Why don't you do it now, and make this the first day of your life?

What do Christ's miracles prove?

The plain teaching of Scripture is that Jesus was God on earth. But God does not expect us to believe on the basis of words alone; instead, he appeals to the evidence of miracles. In a conversation with some hostile people, Jesus freely admitted that his words alone would not be convincing evidence. But there was plenty of evidence for those with eyes to see: the evidence of the work Jesus was doing (John 5:36). Later, he chided the same men for their persistent unbelief. "If you are the Christ, tell us plainly," they demanded. What did he say in reply? "I did tell you, but you do not believe. The miracles I do in my Father's name speak for me. . . . believe the miracles, that you may learn and understand that the Father is in me, and I in the Father" (John 10:25, 38).

Nothing could be plainer that that! He called attention to the miracles he was performing. As the need for miracles arose, he worked them; and he said they proved the truthfulness of his claim to have been sent by the Father. He said virtually the same thing to his followers: "Believe on the evidence of the miracles themselves" (John 14:11).

And yet, there are still those who persist in saying that the miracles of Jesus prove nothing. Lots of people worked miracles, they say. This is true; there were other miracle-workers in the Bible. Jesus raised at least three people from the dead, but he was not the first to do so, nor the last (cf. 1 Kings 17:22; 2 Kings 4:32ff.; Acts 9:40; 20:10. For Christ's raisings from the dead, see Luke 7:14, 15; 8:53, 54; John 11:43, 44). He wasn't even the only one to walk on water. Peter also walked on water (Matthew 14:25-33). Thus, the argument goes, the miracles of Christ don't prove anything.

But such a statement ignores vital differences between the miracles of God's servants such as Elijah and Peter and those of Christ himself. In the first place, they raised people who had been dead for less than a day, in some cases a few minutes. But Lazarus, whom Jesus raised from the dead, had been dead four days (John 11:39). Moreover, Elijah, for one, knew that he himself was unable to raise the dead. He called upon the Lord: "O Lord my God, let this boy's life return to him" (1 Kings 17:21). Jesus, on the other hand, said that he himself was the resurrection and the life. When he prayed, he did so for the sake of the people standing by (John 11:25, 26, 42; cf. 6:6).

The difference between his miracles and those done by prophets and apostles was certainly obvious to witnesses living at the time. The disciples knew that Peter could not walk on water. Peter himself could scarcely believe his own eyes, and in a panic he began to sink. The Lord rescued him, and the effect on the others was amazement. They worshiped him, saying, "Truly you are the Son of God" (Matthew 14:33). Nobody worshiped Peter; they knew he'd have drowned if the Lord hadn't taken hold of him.

The conclusion is inescapable—the miracles of Jesus testify to his deity. Certainly the Apostle John thought so. In fact, he selected a few, described them and some of the conversations that ensued, and presented his work to his generation and to us as evidence of the deity of Christ. Here is what he says near the end of the treatise commonly called The Gospel According to St. John: "Jesus did many other miraculous signs in the presence of his disciples, which are not recorded in this book. But these are written that you may believe that Jesus is the Christ, the Son of God, and that believing you may have life in his name" (20:30, 31).

So there you have it: the miracles were signs, designed to point us to Christ, to help us believe the message, knowing that if we do believe, we have eternal life.

Could Christ have sinned?

To some, this may be an academic question. But even if it were purely academic, it would be of absorbing interest to most Christians (and not only to theologians) for the simple reason that everything about Jesus Christ is of interest to us. As it happens, it is a practical question. In what way? Because Christ's nature—on which the answer hinges—and our assurance of salvation are inseparably linked.

The answer to the question is, Christ could not have sinned. Now I realize that not everyone will be satisfied with such a definite answer. They want proof, which is fair enough. There is proof in the Scriptures, and it may be demonstrated in a syllogism—like this: first, God is holy. He cannot commit sin—which is, by at least one biblical definition, the breaking of God's law (cf. 1 John 3:4). Second, Christ is God. Jesus Christ was God here on earth. This is the substance of New Testament teaching about him. Thus, Jesus could not have sinned.

That may sound too simple for some minds. Nevertheless, if the first two propositions are examined carefully, and are verified, the conclusion is inescapable. Are the first two propositions correct? Take the first—that God is holy. His holiness is one of the first revelations about his character. The Apostle Peter quoted a passage from Leviticus that says, "Be holy, because I am holy," in order to stress the importance of holy living among Christians (1 Peter 1:16; Leviticus 11:44, 45; 19:2; cf. Joshua 24:19; Isaiah 6:3). In the past, as at the present, God has always insisted that those who call themselves his people strive for holiness in life (cf. 2 Timothy 2:19; Numbers 16:5). Holiness is the essence of his nature.

What about Christ? The truth, as revealed in the Bible, is that he is the second person of the Trinity, possessing the very nature of God and all the attributes of God. At his birth in Bethlehem, he added to his divine attributes every human attribute insofar as these were not affected by sin. In other words, he did not receive a fallen human nature. He became one person with two natures, divine and human.

What this means—among other things—is that Jesus was not just like us. True, he had a genuinely human nature. But, unlike ours, his was not fallen, it was not tainted. In his personality there was nothing that could respond to solicitation to evil (cf. James 1:13, 14; John 14:30; 1 John 3:5). Not only so, but unlike us he was also divine. The plain truth is that God cannot be tempted by evil (James 1:13). Thus, there was no part of Christ's nature that could have succumbed to temptation to sin. The answer to the question then is, Jesus could not have sinned. The Lord whom we worship is impeccable—the pure and holy Jesus, a worthy sacrifice for our sins, a fit High Priest to represent us even now.

Why does the Bible put such emphasis on the blood of Jesus Christ?

In dictionaries, *blood* is usually defined as "the fluid, commonly red in vertebrates, which circulates in the heart, arteries, and veins of animals, carrying nourishment and oxygen to all parts of the body. . . ." This is not the only meaning of the word, and dictionaries add to their primary definition: "lifeblood; hence, life," and "taking of life, as deeds of blood." There may be other definitions, but these are the three basic meanings of the word: an essential fluid, life itself, and the taking of life as by murder.

These are also the meanings given to the word by the Bible. Not that the Bible defines words; their meanings are determined by usage, and in the Bible the word *blood* is used in the three ways just given. Examples abound. Take this statement from Leviticus 17:11—"For the life of a creature is in the blood, and I have given it to you to make atonement for yourselves on the altar; it is the blood that makes atonement for one's life." That combines at least two of the three meanings given above, and implies the third: the taking of life (cf. Psalm 26:9; 51:14). In places too numerous to mention, killing is termed the "the shedding of blood."

The significance of this is seen in biblical references to the blood of Christ. Take, for example, 1 John 1:7—"the blood of Jesus, his Son, purifies us from every sin." What does this mean? Well, "the blood of Jesus" is obviously a reference to his blood which was spilled at Calvary—the place of his death. We know, of course, that his blood was a fluid circulating in his body. But *that* blood could not purify anyone; flowing in his body, it kept him alive, but did not help anyone else. Thus, in the reference just cited, the blood of Jesus is shed blood.

This is why some translators use the word "death" instead of "blood." In my judgment this is a mistake. Why? First, the Greek word is "blood," and words should be translated literally whenever possible. Second, "death" is too bland a word. True, in the New Testament there are references to the death of Christ. Paul writes that "Christ died for the ungodly," and he says that we were reconciled to God "through the death of his Son" (Romans 5:6, 10). Moreover, in the celebration commonly called the Lord's Supper or the Communion Service or the Eucharist, we "proclaim the Lord's death until he comes" (1 Corinthians 11:26).

In such passages the term "death" is appropriate. But when the apostles speak of Christ's blood, they do so deliberately, to emphasize a truth that the word "death" cannot convey—that Christ's death was *violent.* Blood is the visible evidence of a life violently ended, as by murder or in warfare. But when used of Christ's death it is also the token of a life *given.* True, it was taken; wicked men murdered him. But the ultimate truth with respect to his death is that he gave his life. Thus, "the blood of Jesus" is his life which he voluntarily gave for us.

The question is, have we availed ourselves of his immense sacrifice? How do we do this? By faith we appropriate that death. When we believe in Christ, his shed blood—i.e., his death—suffices to enable a holy God to forgive us all our sins.

What difference would it make today if Jesus Christ had not risen from the dead?

Christian hymnody is rich with songs about Christ's resurrection. One old favorite goes like this:

The strife is o'er, the battle done;
Now is the Victor's triumph won;
Now be the song of praise begun,—Hallelujah!

The powers of death have done their worst,
But Christ their legions hath dispersed;
Let shouts of holy joy outburst,—Hallelujah!

The theme is joy because of Christ's triumph over the grave.
Another favorite goes like this:

Crown him the Lord of life,
Who triumphed over the grave,
And rose victorious in the strife
For those he came to save.
His glories now we sing
Who died and rose on high,
Who died eternal life to bring,
And lives that death may die.

Here there is the additional thought of the benefit of Christ's resurrection for believers—eternal life; and it is this, of course, that really inspires the holy joy of the first hymn.

But supposing Christ did not rise from the dead. Then what?

Not everyone believes that Jesus Christ did in fact rise from the dead, and for those who do not, our question is silly. If someone said he could prove that Christ did not not rise from the dead, it would not affect them much; they have always lived their lives as if he had not risen.

Nevertheless, the truth of his resurrection does affect them, whether they know it or not, for it is a guarantee of their judgment. The Apostle Paul emphasized this point when talking to a few would-be philosophers in Athens. Here's what Paul said: "Now [God] commands all people everywhere to repent. For he has set a day when he will judge the world with justice by the man he has appointed. He has given proof of this to all men by raising him from the dead" (Acts 17:31). Do we get the message? Christ's resurrection is proof that God will someday judge the world. This is why the fact is unpopular in some quarters.

As for us Christians, if Jesus Christ did not rise from the dead, as we all believe he did, it would make all the difference in the world. The Apostle Paul explained that if Christ did not rise from the dead, nobody will. Those who have died are finished, *kaput*. The grave ends it all. If Christ did not rise from the dead, there is no such thing as eternal life. We just spin out our lives like rational animals who have no significance. Our deaths would be no more meaningful than the death of a cat run down by a car.

Paul also said that if Christ did not rise, Christian preachers are all false witnesses, since the keystone truth of their preaching is the resurrection of Christ. Furthermore, all their converts are dupes, which is a fancy word for dopes, if Christ was not raised from the dead. Their faith in God is worthless.

Now that's pretty strong language, but it came from the Apostle Paul. You can check it for yourself in 1 Corinthians 15. He said that if Christ did not rise, then Christians are of all men most to be pitied. Lots of people already pity us, as if we were mentally deficient for believing that Christ did indeed rise from the dead. But of course they have never investigated the evidence for the resurrection. It can be said with certainty that no historical event of that period comes to us as strongly documented. But all the evidence in the world cannot convince a man against his will.

For those of us who believe, Christ's resurrection is the source of our hope. A living hope, Peter called it: "In his great mercy he has given us new birth into a living hope through the resurrection of Jesus Christ from the dead" (1 Peter 1:3).

Why did Jesus not know the time of his return?

There is at least one verse in the Bible that seems to say that Jesus did not know everything. It is often quoted by those who deny or question his omniscience. The verse is Mark 13:32—"No one knows about that day or hour, not even the angels in heaven, nor the Son, but only the Father." The reference is to the second coming of Christ, and the verse seems to say that Christ himself does not know when he will return.

Does it really say that? If so, how do we account for the various passages that prove that Christ was God on Earth? God knows everything; he even knows what we are thinking, and he knows the future before it happens (cf. Psalm 94:11; 139:2; Isaiah 46:10; 48:5).

This was true of Jesus. The testimony of those who knew him best is that he knew what men were thinking. On more than one occasion he answered their questions before they could articulate them (cf. Luke 5:22; 9:47; John 2:24, 25). Not only so, he also predicted the future and, with the exception of one item, everything he said would happen, happened. The exception is his return—for which he set no dates. The fact that he has not yet returned says only that insufficient time has elapsed. If Christ's prediction that he would be crucified, would stay in the tomb three days, and would rise again came true, and if his prediction that Jerusalem would be sacked within a generation of his own crucifixion came true, there is every reason to believe that his promise to return will be fulfilled (cf. Matthew 20:18, 19; John 13:1, 3, 11; 18:4).

But why didn't he know the time of his return? Was he genuinely ignorant? The disciples didn't think so; they were convinced that he knew everything (cf. John 16:30; 21:17). Then why the exception? The answer is, he *chose* not to know. Whether this means that he genuinely did not know, or merely refused to utilize knowledge that was his as God the Son may be an unanswerable question. What matters is that he was able to choose not to know something.

This is puzzling, to be sure. But there are analogies in Scripture. For example, in a place where our Lord talks about Heaven, he says that many who will be excluded will protest that they were his disciples and should be admitted. They will say that in his name they prophesied, drove out demons, and even performed miracles. How will he reply? Here are his own words: "Then I will tell them plainly, 'I never knew you. Away from me, you evildoers' " (Matthew 7:23).

"I never knew you." Yet he knows all men. What does it mean? That he doesn't really know them? No; it means that he will not accept fake Christians. Similarly, the verse that says he does not know the day or hour of the second coming means only that he *does not will to know* the time, does not set the time, and does not act upon knowledge of the date. As he told his followers, setting dates is the Father's prerogative (Acts 1:7).

It isn't our concern, either. Fixing dates or speculating about the time of Christ's return is a silly, even sinful waste of time. It makes far more sense to busy ourselves with the business of loving as Christians, ready for the Lord's return whenever it may please the Father to send him (Luke 12:40; Matthew 24:42-44).

What does the word Messiah mean?

The dictionary indicates this word's Hebrew and Aramaic roots and gives the literal, original meaning: "anointed." It also gives three current usages of the word: (1) the expected king and deliverer of the Jews; (2) Jesus; and (3) a professed or accepted leader of some hope or cause.

It's clear to me that Webster went to a Bible dictionary or some other tool used by Bible students to find the meaning of this word. The dictionary is right; the word does indeed mean "anointed" in its original form, and it is used in the Hebrew Bible (that is, the Old Testament) to denote the Jews' expected king. The hope of a coming Messiah permeates the Old Testament. In fact, according to some accounts there are as many as 450 references to him—in the opinion of the rabbis who lived in the pre-Christian era.

The word *Messiah* is found in the New Testament in a couple of places (John 1:41; 4:29). A man called Andrew spent a night listening to Jesus, then hurried off to find his own brother, Peter. "We have found the Messiah," he said. And in the text where that statement is given there is a note, included in the manuscript of the Gospel according to John, which says simply that the word *Messiah* is *Christ* in Greek. So when you hear the word *Messiah,* you know it is Christ, or a variation of it, in most Western languages.

Knowing what the word means is important, but the information is wasted unless we realize that Jesus is indeed the Messiah—that is, the Christ. He claimed to be, you know. When he asked his friends who they thought he was, Peter spoke up for all of them and said, "You are the Christ, the Son of the living God" (John 6:69). You are the Messiah, the Anointed One; you are the Son of the living God, Peter said. Did Jesus deny it? Not at all. In fact, he told Peter that God had revealed it to Peter; he hadn't figured it out in his own head (Matthew 16:15, 16). In saying that God had revealed to Peter the fact that Jesus was indeed the Christ, our Lord claimed to be the Messiah, the Son of God.

If so, it makes a difference whether we believe or not. As for me, I believe. I believe that Jesus is the Christ, the Son of the living God. I believe that he is Lord, and I believe he has forgiven me all my sins through the merits of his blood which was shed for me.

How about you?

Who is greater, Christ or God?

We Christians are sometimes puzzled by biblical statements that seem to contradict each other. Some of the sayings of Christ himself fall into this class. For example, he said, "I and the Father are one," and he also said "the Father is greater than I" (John 10:30; 14:28). Is this a real or merely apparent contradiction? The question is, is the Son equal with the Father, or isn't he?

The answer is, he is equal with the Father. Then how do we explain our Lord's own statement that "the Father is greater"? As is so often the case, the solution to the apparent contradiction lies in study of the context in which the problem text occurs, and in comparison with other passages.

Taking these in reverse order, it is clear from Christ's statement that he and the Father were one, and from an earlier assertion that the Father intended that all should honor the Son just as they honor the Father, that Jesus felt himself to be equal with the Father (John 10:30; 5:22, 23). Jesus was (and, of course, still is) God—which, by definition, precludes the idea of inferiority to any other being.

Now for the context in which we find Christ's acknowledgment that the Father was greater than he: Jesus is telling his followers that he must leave them. "I am going away and I am coming back to you," he says. And then he says something strange: "If you loved me, you would be glad that I am going to the Father. . . ." Why should they be glad? "Because the Father is greater than I." Jesus clearly meant that for him it would be better to leave them and return to the Father.

But why should the fact that the Father was greater make it better for him to return to the Father? Because the Father's relative superiority lay in the fact that he was in Heaven, whereas the Son was on Earth. The Father was the object of glory and honor; the Son was despised and rejected by men. In his prayer—recorded in John 17—Christ asked his Father to glorify him with the glory which he had with the Father before the world began (verse 5). In becoming man, Christ had forfeited—temporarily—that glory which was his as the second person of the Godhead. The Father had not laid aside his glory, and in this sense he was greater than the Son.

Was Christ's prayer answered? Yes, it was. The Apostle Peter explains, "He (i.e., Christ) was chosen before the creation of the world, but was revealed in these last times for your sake. Through him you believed in God, who raised him from the dead and glorified him, and so your faith and hope are in God" (1 Peter 1:20, 21).

The fact is, God the Son is God, equal with God the Father and the Holy Spirit, both now and forever.

Did Jesus worship God?

Many people who are not Christians agree that Jesus Christ was a good man. But they don't know what they are talking about; they haven't seriously thought about the question, nor have they—for the most part—examined the documents that tell us what he was really like. They say what they just *assume* to be true. If you were to ask them if they think Jesus was religious, they might reply that he was indeed; he was, they add, what is popularly termed a "religious genius"—whatever that might be. They assume—without ever checking to see if it is true—that he was very pious and worshiped God in earnest.

The truth is, Jesus did *not* worship God. True, when Satan attempted to persuade Jesus to worship him, Jesus replied that the Scriptures say "Worship the Lord your God and serve him only" (Luke 4:8; Deuteronomy 6:13). But he himself did *not* worship God. It is vain to argue that he practiced what he preached; that argument is not always valid. For instance, he told Nicodemus that he had to be born again. Yet he himself did not have a fallen nature, as did Nicodemus and everybody else in the world. Consequently he needed no second birth.

Why didn't Jesus worship God? The answer is plain: he himself was (and is) God. How can God worship himself? He can't! And the truth is, there is no verse in the Bible that says Jesus worshiped God. True, he *prayed* to his Father, and he *gave thanks*. He also *praised* God, as in that passage in Matthew's Gospel where he says, "I praise you, Father, Lord of heaven and earth, because you have hidden these things from the wise and learned, and revealed them to little children" (Matthew 11:25; cf. 26:42; Luke 3:21; 5:16; 6:12; John 17:11, 20). But at no time did he worship the Father.

Instead, he taught men living in his times, and he teaches us now in the Bible, that *we* ought to worship God. Furthermore, he tells us how to worship. "A time is coming and has now come," he says, "when the true worshipers will worship the Father in spirit and in truth, for they are the kind of worshipers the Father seeks" (John 4:23, 24).

In view of this statement, it is significant that Jesus received worship from his followers. No other fact could more emphatically underline the biblical teaching that Jesus was God on Earth than his willingness to receive the worship which he himself said was due to God alone. "Worship the Lord your God," he said. After the resurrection his friends frequently fell at his feet and worshiped him, and he did not stop them. None expressed their conviction more forcibly than Thomas who, seeing the nail wounds in Christ's hands and the spear wound in his side, said what evidently became a credal statement: "My Lord and my God" (John 20:28; 1 Corinthians 12:3).

Did Jesus rebuke him for blasphemy? No. Instead, he pronounced a blessing on all who believe the same thing, though without benefit of material evidence—which Thomas demanded, and received. "Blessed are those," he said, "who have not seen and yet have believed" (verse 29).

Would a truly good man act and talk like that? Not unless he was in fact what his friends believed him to be—God in the flesh. That is what I believe him to be; for me personally the logical alternative—that Jesus was a self-deluded and deluding megalomaniac—is inadmissible. And for those who sincerely seek after God and examine the records, there is only one acceptable conclusion: that Jesus is God. He did not worship God; instead, he received the worship of his creatures. He still does. Are you a worshiper? If not, you'll have to answer to him for your failure to do so.

Do the Gospels give facts or legends about Jesus Christ?

More than fifty-five years ago a writer for the *Manchester Guardian* explained that "the primary office of a newspaper is the gathering of news." "Comment is free," he observed, "but facts are sacred" (May 6, 1926). Good newspapers still subscribe to the view that facts are sacred. A columnist may express virtually any opinion he likes, provided he keeps the facts straight. Facts are facts, as the saying goes.

Someone has said that modern science trains the mind to an exact and impartial analysis of the facts. This may be one of science's objectives, since science is indeed concerned with facts. But the truth is, many scientists are highly selective in the facts they are willing to analyze. Certain historical facts—in particular, biblical facts—are splendidly ignored by men of science and others for whom the facts of the gospel are awkward. The trick is to decide in advance that certain things can't happen; they just *can't* happen, therefore they didn't happen—no matter how much evidence may exist in support of their factualness.

In addition to those who ignore biblical facts which call for attention, there are those who set out to reduce to myth the "irreducible and stubborn facts" (Alfred North Whitehead) of the gospel. The ease with which they do this amazes those who know their Bibles well. Several methods are used, all designed to invalidate the historical accuracy of the Gospels. For example, critics ignore the testimony of Christians living in the first two or three centuries—as if it were easier now, in the twentieth century, to determine exactly what happened in Palestine in the first century than it was at that very time!

Another trick is to assume—without a shred of evidence in support of the assumption—that the early Christians recreated Christ. That is, that the Christ they worshiped was the product of their imaginations rather than reality; the real thing, the theory goes, was just a Jewish peasant whom the Romans executed. This flies in the face of all the evidence available—evidence presented by men of unquestioned integrity who lived at the time and who, with one possible exception, sacrificed their lives in defense of the truth they proclaimed. Their writings attest to their character; it is inconceivable that such men could have willfully distorted the life of Christ.

Yet if the picture they present and the conversations they record are not true to reality, they must have willfully corrupted the truth. Why is this the case? Because every other fact in the Gospel narratives—i.e., facts about names and places—are verifiable. Not one of the apostles has ever been proven inaccurate in his material. Thus, the historical Jesus of their narratives, and the Jesus whom Christians worshiped as Lord are the same person. The Christ who we worship is not a theological construct, as unbelievers like to think.

The only explanation for the existence of the early church is the actualness of the Gospel narratives. There is no other explanation. The apostles could not have invented the story, and by themselves they could not have supplied the dynamic that called the church existence. The only valid explanation for the existence of the New Testament and the church it describes is factualness of the account. The Lord whom early Christians worshiped was real; he lived, worked, died, rose from the dead, and ascended into Heaven exactly as the narrative says he did.

What this means for you and me should be obvious: faith in this person makes us Christians; refusal to believe, on the other hand, separates us from the grace of God. It dooms us to the lost eternity to which we are even now headed.

What is so important about the teachings of Jesus Christ?

Jesus was the greatest physician who ever lived, and naturally mobs followed him wherever he went. Those who were well brought their sick relatives to see him, and he healed them. The cures where instant, and none of his patients had relapses. But a country never runs out of sick people, and before long huge crowds accompanied him as he toured Galilee. They made it difficult for him and his friends to find time to eat. Not only so, but they threatened to divert him from the more serious business of teaching and preaching the Word of God. Their constant clamor was for the healing of their bodies, not their souls. So he climbed a mountain and sat down on a level place. His disciples followed him up the hill, and when they also had seated themselves he began to teach them. What he said was infinitely better than what he did for human bodies; his words were sweet as honey to those who had made the effort to climb the mountain.

He taught them great truths in what is usually called the Sermon on the Mount. The "sermon" was a kind of manifesto—that is, a public declaration of the true nature of the kingdom he had come to establish. His followers needed enlightenment, since many of them evidently assumed that he would found it on force—as is the case with most world kingdoms. Their prophets, notably Daniel, spoke of such a kingdom, but the time for that sort of kingdom was not yet ripe (Daniel 2:44). Jesus had come to establish a spiritual kingdom, not a political or military entity (Luke 17:20, 21; John 18:36). Hence, the Sermon on the Mount.

It should be observed that he "lived" the Sermon before he taught it. His opponents were great teachers, but they didn't practice what they preached—like many a person since their time (Matthew 23:1-3). Jesus practiced what he preached before he preached it. He was consistent, too. Near the end, certain bitter antagonists said, "Who are you?" (John 8:25). "Just what I have been claiming all along," was his answer.

He also claimed that his words (including the Sermon on the Mount) were his Father's words; they were the very words of God. He said, "There is a judge for the one who rejects me and does not accept my words; that very word which I spoke will condemn him at the last day. For I did not speak of my own accord, but the Father who sent me commanded me what to say and how to say it. I know that his command leads to eternal life. So what I say is just what the Father has told me to say" (John 12:48-50; cf. 17:8, 14).

Nothing could be more explicit than that statement. God the Father told him to say what he actually said in the Sermon on the Mount. Those words lead to eternal life, but there is judgment for the one who rejects Jesus and does not accept his words. In my thinking, there is no more solemn thought than that!

Christ loved the church and gave himself up for her. (Ephesians 5:25)

. . . God's household, which is the church of the living God, the pillar and foundation of the truth. (1 Timothy 3:15)

Let us not give up meeting together, as some are in the habit of doing, but let us encourage one another—and all the more as you see the Day approaching. (Hebrews 10:25)

Christ is the head of the body, the church. (Colossians 1:18)

8/WHAT IS THE CHURCH, AND WHAT IS ITS PURPOSE?

Some people commit themselves to numerous church duties; others avoid the church altogether. We each need to discover for ourselves what the church is supposed to be like and where we fit in.

What is the church?

Martin Luther once said, "A seven-year-old child knows what the church is: holy believers and lambs who hear the voice of their shepherd (John 10:10)." In Luther's times, seven-year-old children may have known more than they appear to know in these days. Still, a child might give that answer even today, in which case he would be doing quite well indeed. Basically, the church is indeed those who have believed in Jesus Christ and now follow him.

Bible students often prefer more precise definitions of the church, according to which it may be defined as the body of Christ, or the fellowship of saints. The rub is that non-Christians don't always know what Christians mean by these terms. Take the two definitions in reverse order. What is meant by the fellowship of saints? That expression combines two great truths concerning the church. First, it is composed of true believers—i.e., those who have surrendered in faith to our Lord. This is what is meant by the word *saints*. The Bible does not use the word to describe extraordinary believers with halos over their heads; it uses it to speak of you and me—all who have made an irrevocable commitment to Christ. So the church is composed of true believers, and no one else.

The word *fellowship* is our English equivalent of the Latin *communion* and emphasizes the great truth that the church is made up of many believers. When you make your commitment to Christ, you find yourself a vital part of a living organism—not just a member of a paper organization. So the church is people—a special kind of people, who share a common life through their personal relationship with Jesus Christ, their Lord.

This is what is meant by the fairly familiar term, *the body of Christ* (see 1 Corinthians 12:12, 13). The Apostle Paul liked the metaphor of the body; it stresses the great truth that the members live only in virtue of their relationship to the head, which is Christ. Furthermore, as said already, their relationship with Christ binds them together, even as the various members of a body—arms, legs, ears, and everything else—are parts of a single unity. Union with Christ and union with each other—that's what the term means.

Obviously, we aren't talking about a building with a steeple, and we're not talking about any particular denomination. Local churches, no matter what their denominational label, are simply parts of the whole. No congregation or groups of congregations is *the* church. So we come back to the definition given by Luther's seven-year-old child. What is the church? It is holy believers and lambs who hear the voice of their shepherd.

Are you part of the church?

Why should I attend church?

In these times, former church-attenders are staying away in droves. They wash the car on Sunday or play golf. Some just stay home and read the paper or sleep in. If you ask them why they don't go to church, they may tell you it is a waste of time—the sermons are a bore or the entire service is irrelevant to their needs. Irrelevant—that's a popular word. Or they might feel like the writer Robert Louis Stevenson who believed that every man is his own doctor of divinity *(An Inland Voyage)*. He's the one who said, "I have been to church today and am now depressed."

Going to church should not be depressing; instead, it should be meaningful and helpful, as it unquestionably was in the first century and many times since. Are there any genuine values left in going to church?

The answer depends to a certain extent on the church in question. For me, attendance at a church where there is little or no emphasis on the study of the Bible would be of minimal value. I like the occasional book review, and I can take my fair share of political talks. But I don't want to go to church to hear them. In church I prefer hearing the preaching or teaching of the Word of God. It is this that strengthens me as a Christian.

There are, of course, other values in attendance at church. One obvious value is the warmth and strength communicated by other Christians. Few if any of us have what it takes to survive in isolation from other Christians. Christians in Angola often point out that an ember pulled from the fire soon cools off and goes out. It's the same with Christians. Withdraw from your fellow-believers and you will soon grow cold in heart. And there is no heart as cold as the heart of a backslidden Christian.

The same Angolan Christians say that one straw doesn't make a broom. Bunch many straws together, however, and you have a useful tool. It's the same with Christians. Stand alone, and you're weak and ineffective. Get together with other believers and you become strong and useful—strong enough to sweep a lot of dirt out of the community if you so direct your energies.

Maybe this is why the Bible warns us not to forsake the assembling of ourselves together (Hebrews 10:25). The least we can do by attending church regularly is to encourage and help one another. We also cast our vote in favor of the truth the church stands for. Come to think of it, failure to attend is not ony a tacit refusal to support the church, it is a vote in favor of its death. I think I'd rather crawl to church than vote for boarding it up.

If you could make one change in your church, what would it be?

I don't know. Catch me at any other time and I might be able to suggest half a dozen needed changes. In my present mood I can't think of any, except perhaps the time we meet together on Sundays.

And even that is unimportant to me; it's a question of personal convenience, hardly worth mentioning.

Actually, I like current arrangements in the church I attend; I would not make any changes, except on an experimental basis. For example, we could try different things at the prayer meeting in an attempt to get more of the Christians present to participate. Or we could change the format of the Sunday morning preaching service. But these are not really changes—i.e., they do not affect the fundamental expressions of the church's life and purpose in the world today.

What I'd strive for would be improvements in what we are now doing, not drastic changes. I believe in regular attendance at church—for several good reasons—and would like to see attendance improved. Those of us who call ourselves Christians should make every effort to be in our places at the prayer meeting, meetings for teaching, etc. The early Christians met together regularly (see Acts 2:42) to listen to the apostles' teaching, for fellowship, to break bread together, and for prayer. Each church needs a program designed to provide these needs, and every believer ought to support such a program by being present at the meetings.

If such a program already exists, no serious alterations are needed. All that is needed is a little more zeal for the Lord than most of us manifest. We have a positive genius for thinking of excuses for cutting meetings, as if attendance were a bore rather than an opportunity to help someone or, as so often happens, to be helped.

By itself, attending meetings more faithfully won't solve all a congregation's problems. But it is a start, a good one. It is often the first step toward changing, not something abstract like a church, but the people who really make it what it is.

Do not worry about tomorrow, for tomorrow will worry about itself. Each day has enough trouble of its own. (Matthew 6:34)

Do not be anxious about anything, but in everything, by prayer and petition, with thanksgiving, present your requests to God. And the peace of God, which transcends all understanding, will guard your hearts and minds in Christ Jesus. (Philippians 4:6, 7)

I eagerly expect and hope that I will in no way be ashamed, but will have sufficient courage so that now as always Christ will be exalted in my body, whether by life or by death. For to me, to live is Christ and to die is gain. (Philippians 1:20, 21)

Even though I walk through the valley of the shadow of death, I will fear no evil, for you are with me; your rod and your staff, they comfort me. (Psalm 23:4)

9/WHAT WILL THE FUTURE BRING?

We all have great hopes for the future—and great fears. We wish we could unroll the scroll of time and see what lies ahead, but we know we can't. Will God will be able to help us with whatever comes?

Is our world getting better or worse?

The *Internationale* is Communism's rallying song to the wretched of the earth to build a better world.

> Arise, ye prisoners of starvation,
>   Arise, ye wretched of the earth,
> For justice thunders condemnation—
>   A better world's in birth.   (Eugene Pottier)

Is the world really getting better than it was, or is it worse?

More recently the Broadway play *Hair* popularized a song entitled "Aquarius":

> When the moon is in the seventh house,
> And Jupiter aligns with Mars:
> Then Peace will guide the planets
> And Love will steer the stars.
> This is the dawning of the Age of Aquarius.

The notion behind the words is derived from astrology, according to which a new star-age is about to begin. Everything will be better, it is said. A new world is coming.

It sounds great, but is it true? Many thinking people think the world is actually getting worse; in fact, for many of the world's intellectuals the world's prospects are so bad that life is hardly worth living. So the recurring question is, is the world getting better or worse?

I wonder sometimes if it is really changing either way. Many centuries ago, a writer said, "What has been will be again, and what has been done will be done again; there is nothing new under the sun" (Ecclesiastes 1:9). But maybe he'd change his tune if he were living today. The world is much more densely populated than in ancient times, and as a consequence there is greater pollution with its attendant miseries. In that fellow's time, nobody had to breathe smog or post "No Swimming" signs on the beaches. The world is also technologically advanced, and while this means creature-comforts such as inner-spring mattresses and TV dinners, it has its price to pay. We run the daily risk of being squashed under a passing automobile or, if we stay in bed, of burning to death due to a faulty electrical connection. So if the Preacher were editing Ecclesiastes for modern readers, he might say that things are worse than they were in the good old days.

Folks with a little knowledge of history might argue the point. They'd point to ancient wars like the Crusades, or pestilence and plague that occasionally wiped out half the population of a city or even a nation, or institutionalized slavery, or child labor in, say, Dickens's times, and they'd insist that the modern world is better than it was. It all depends upon the viewpoint.

From the standpoint of human character, not much has changed. There have always been men of God, such as Job and Abraham and others too numerous to mention. And there have always been evil men—worthless fellows, the Bible calls them. These are the majority. No device has ever been found to eliminate the tendency, even in good men, toward degeneracy. Various controls have been imposed over the centuries, but none has been completely successful. Men may change, but mankind does not change. Hence, we are as capable of cruelty now as in mankind's darkest hour. We are no better than our ancestors; we are as capable of evil as they.

However, the Bible predicts a worldwide expression of evil in the future. "There will be terrible times in the last days," Paul wrote. "People will be lovers of themselves, lovers of money, boastful, proud, abusive, disobedient to their parents, ungrateful, unholy, without love, unforgiving, slanderous, without self-control, brutal, not lovers of the good, treacherous, rash, conceited, lovers of pleasure rather than lovers of God" (2 Timothy 3:1-4). He also foretold the coming of a world ruler whose coming would be "in accordance with the work of Satan . . . [who] in every sort of evil deceives those who are perishing" (2 Thessalonians 2:9, 10).

Clearly, there will be an unprecedented intensification of evil at the end of the age. So while it may be hard to decide whether the world is getting better or worse, we know that it *will* get worse. Much worse.

Can we ever accomplish world peace?

No, there is no way we can achieve world peace. Human nature is so incurably self-seeking that nothing short of divine intervention in the affairs of the world can ever bring about a state of global peace. Even apart from the Word of God, this should be evident to anyone who studies history. Since the time men began to record what they were doing, the world has never known a prolonged period of peace on earth. There have been literally thousands of wars since the beginning of history.

Some folks think that man is a product of evolution. In his primitive stages, they feel, he was naturally aggressive and warlike. Hence, the many wars of the past. In my thinking, this is hogwash. If man has evolved at all, he has evolved downward. There is no evidence whatsoever for thinking that human nature today is a whit better than it was 10,000 years ago. In fact, no modern government comes even near equaling the ancient Hebrew theocracy, as it was called, for fairness. For its members, at least, that nation guaranteed considerably more liberty, justice, and brotherhood than is available in the world today.

As for wars, nowadays there are as many as ever in the past. We are obviously as mean as ever, and wars simply reflect the inner wars that rage in every man's soul. Someday there will be peace. But it won't be the product of some politician's fertile mind. It will be imposed on the nations of the world—forcibly imposed by God's Son, Jesus Christ. The second Psalm is a divine statement on that subject.

In my view, the most important thing any individual can do is make his personal peace with God. How? By coming on his knees in faith to Jesus Christ. Then, the Bible says, while there may be no peace anywhere else in the world, there will be peace in your soul.

Is the world coming to an end?

No, not in the immediate future. And yet, someday this old world will come to an end—a catastrophic end, according to the Apostle Peter. He said the present heavens and earth are being "reserved for fire, kept for the day of judgment and destruction of ungodly men." Peter explained that when that day of destruction comes, "the heavens will disappear with a roar; the elements will be destroyed by fire, and the earth and everything in it will be laid bare" (2 Peter 3:7, 10).

Three facts should be kept in mind. First, the theory that the universe is winding down cannot explain the coming destruction. The cosmic explosions of the future will be an act of God. He has announced his intention of purging a cosmos spoiled by sin. So the end of the present world will be an act of God.

The second fact concerns his timetable. The fiery purging of the heavens and the Earth to which Peter referred will not take place until the end of a long period of time usually called the Millennium. Reference to this may be found in Revelation 20:1-6, as well as in literally scores of other passages. The Millenium or 1000-year period of peace will end in a rebellion fomented by Satan, whom God will cast into the lake of fire (Revelation 20:7-10). That judgment on Satan will be followed by the final judgment of the lost souls of the world's history, from Cain to the last man to reject God's mercy. And then, when this is done, God will purge the heavens and the earth with fire.

The third fact concerns the new heavens and the new Earth that God will create to replace the present cosmos. Isaiah predicted it (i.e., God predicted it through his servant Isaiah) in his writings (65:17; 66:22); Paul referred to it (Romans 8:21); and John confirmed it in the Apocalypse (21:1ff.). So there's a new world coming, which—to use Peter's phrase—is "the home of righteousness" (2 Peter 3:13). John said that "nothing impure will ever enter it, nor will anyone who does what is shameful or deceitful, but only those whose names are written in the Lamb's book of life" (Revelation 21:27).

And this brings us to still another fact—questions about the end of the world are relatively unimportant. Vastly more important to us is the question of our soul's salvation. Are we ready for death? This is the crucial question. The world won't come to an end in our time, but death is fast approaching. Are we ready for it? Are we ready for the new world God is preparing for those whose sins have been forgiven? Preparation is possible only through a personal act of faith in Jesus Christ. The big question is whether we have put our trust in him, and so prepared ourselves for death.

Do you believe that Jesus is coming back?

I believe that Jesus will return because the Bible clearly indicates it. Because I believe the Bible is the Word of God, I must accept it in its entirety. In fact, everyone who believes the Bible is the Word of God is logically compelled to believe that Jesus will come back.

Does the Bible actually teach this? Yes, it does.

Jesus himself said he would come back. In the last week of his life before the crucifixion, he gathered his special friends together and said this: "Do not let your hearts be troubled. Trust in God; trust also in me. In my Father's house are many rooms; if it were not so, I would have told you. I am going there to prepare a place for you. And if I go and prepare a place for you, I will come back and take you to be with me that you also may be where I am" (John 14:1-4). Could any promise be plainer?

Some may argue that he was using figurative or poetic language.

They are mistaken. All his talk about leaving them was literal truth; he even died precisely as he said he would die, and he was resurrected literally even as he said he would be. His promise to come back must be taken as literally as were all his other statements.

His friends certainly believed he meant what he said, and they understood him to have said he would return. Their impression was confirmed in their minds when he departed from them. While they were watching him ascend to Heaven, two men in white stood beside them and said, "Men of Galilee, why do you stand here looking into the sky? This same Jesus, who has been taken from you into heaven, will come back in the same way you have seen him go into heaven" (Acts 1:10). They believed it, and they spent their lives believing it and teaching others to believe it. Take those people in a city called Thessalonica—miles and miles away from Palestine. The Apostle Paul taught them not only to turn from idols to serve the living God, but also to wait for his Son from Heaven, whom he raised from the dead—that is, Jesus, who delivers us from the wrath to come (1 Thessalonians 1:9, 10).

If you don't believe in him, there's not much sense in waiting for him, because he won't come for you. You'll be left behind. But that's another subject—an unspeakably sad one.

Can Christ really return at any moment?

A question frequently pondered by Christians who wish to know what God has planned for them is, are there any prophecies yet to be fulfilled before Christ comes for his church? Must something happen before Christ's return, to clear the way for him?

The answer is no. In my understanding of New Testament teaching about the return of the Lord, the Christian's hope is the *imminent* coming of Christ. I emphasize the word *imminent* because it can take place at any time. Before his passion our Lord assured his disciples that he would return; he didn't say *when,* but the evidence of the Scriptures is that they expected him to come back at any moment. Apparently they were careful to distinguish between his promise to come for them, and his return in judgment. In my thinking, the confusion in many minds about the subject derives from a failure to make that same distinction. To put it another way, the promise to come for his disciples (often called the Rapture of the church), which we find in the upper room discourse, should not be confused with the discourse on the Mount of Olives. In the one, Jesus spoke to his friends in the first person and promised to come back for them. In the other, he discussed events scheduled to happen considerably later.

Several important passages indicate that Christ's people will accompany him when he comes to the Earth in power and glory. "God will bring with Jesus those who have fallen asleep in him" (1 Thessalonians 4:14) is an example. Check Colossians 3:4 for another, and also Revelation 19:14. If this is true, then Christ must come for them first. Those who have died will be raised, and those who are still alive when the Lord comes will be caught up, as Paul explains, to meet the Lord in the air. He adds that we shall be always with the Lord, and that includes his public, glorious return to the earth.

Certainly the great Apostle Paul lived in expectation of Christ's return at any moment. In a sense it didn't matter to him whether the Lord came in his lifetime or later. What mattered most was that he lived for Christ. He was quite realistic about death and dying, being willing to die and willing also to live and labor for the Master. But his hope was the return of Christ. "Our citizenship is in heaven," he wrote. "And we eagerly await a Savior from there, the Lord Jesus Christ" (Philippians 3:20). He communicated that hope to his converts. Consequently, the new Christians in Thessalonica not only served the living and true God, whom they had found through Paul's preaching, but also waited for his Son from Heaven (1 Thessalonians 1:10).

As far as I can tell, there is no instruction in the New Testament for Christians to wait for an event; they are to wait for a person— Jesus Christ. Hebrews 9 is a reference to his return. He will appear, the passage says, "to those who are waiting for him" (verse 28). James exhorted his believing friends to be patient "until the Lord's coming" (James 5:7).

Obviously, then, there is no unfulfilled prophecy awaiting fulfillment before he comes. If there were, how could we wait for him? We'd watch and wait for an event of some sort, instead of for him.

But waiting for him is the essence of Christian living. Like those

Christians in the first century, we also "turned to God from idols"—twentieth-century, American idols—"to serve the living and true God, and to wait for his Son from heaven, whom he raised from the dead—Jesus, who rescues us from the coming wrath" (1 Thessalonians 1:9, 10).

Will loved ones be reunited in Heaven?

In his poem titled, "Break, Break, Break," Lord Tennyson longs for ". . . the touch of a vanish'd hand, / And the sound of a voice that is still!" And on a tombstone in ancient Thessalonica there was the inscription, "After death, no returning; in the grave, no seeing again." Both the poem and the inscription on the tombstone express the grief of the bereaved who have no hope whatsoever of seeing their loved ones again. But Christ gives his followers hope. Paul explained that "Christ Jesus . . . has destroyed death and has brought life and immortality to light through the gospel" (2 Timothy 1:10). Does that include the hope of seeing loved ones again?

Yes,—assuming that the loved ones in question were believers while on Earth. Otherwise, there can be no reunion in Heaven. The Bible says, "whoever believes in the Son (i.e., Jesus Christ) has eternal life, but whoever rejects the Son will not see life, for God's wrath remains on him" (John 3:36). It's as simple as that. When he was on earth, Jesus Christ was a divider of families. He admitted as much. ". . . I have come to turn 'a man against his father,' " he said, " 'and a daughter against her mother, and a daughter-in-law against her mother-in-law—a man's enemies will be members of his own household' " (Matthew 10:35, 36). He divided families by attracting some members to himself, so that they became his friends and disciples. Others hated him and rejected him. Obviously, families like that cannot be reunited in Heaven. They were divided in spirit on Earth, and they will be separated eternally after death. That prospect is unspeakably sad.

As for reunited families, their joy will be complete. But relationships in Heaven will be changed. A man will no longer have his former wife as wife, and vice versa, because in Heaven there is no marriage. Jesus said, "The people of this age marry and are given in marriage. But those who are considered worthy of taking part in that age (i.e., the future world) and in the resurrection from the dead will neither marry nor be given in marriage" (Luke 20:34, 35). Consequently, it is a mistake to think of Heaven as an extension of Earth. In Heaven there are no tidy little families consisting of Papa and Mama and one or more children. Everything will be changed.

What kind of relationships will there be? In the passage already cited, the Lord said that those who make it to Heaven "are like the angels. They are God's children, since they are children of the resurrection" (verse 36). The old relationships depended upon birth; everybody was somebody's son or daughter. But in Heaven there is no death, and hence no need to replenish population losses. Everyone there owes his life to God; he is nobody else's son or daughter or, for that matter, father or mother. Everybody stands in direct relationship to God, as one of his children. Everybody belongs to God.

So, while the believing members of a family will indeed be reunited in Heaven, the old relationships will not continue. They will be changed, replaced by something infinitely better—a direct relationship to God, and a brotherhood that embraces everyone who has ever loved God from every tribe and nation in every generation since the world began.

Will we recognize each other in Heaven?

Hope is one of God's greatest gifts to Christians. Before we became Christians, we were without hope. Not hopeless, to be sure, yet without the hope given to us as a gift when we trusted Christ (cf. Ephesians 2:12; 1:18). The apostles liked to talk about our hope. Peter said God has given us new birth into a living hope, and Paul said we were saved "in" or "unto" the hope of many things, including the redemption of our bodies (1 Peter 1:3; Romans 8:20, 23). This is a great hope; these aging bodies share in God's plan for our future. But this brings up a question. If we will have bodies in Heaven, will we recognize each other there?

We shall indeed know one another, including those whom we knew on Earth and those whom we did not know. Recognition will be immediate, without recourse to formal introductions or the use of name tags.

Now it must be admitted that there is no specific text of Scripture to prove this. The Bible does not say flatly, "You will recognize each other as soon as you see them." But this is a reasonable inference from a number of passages. For example, in the case of the rich man and Lazarus (Luke 16), after death the rich man recognized Lazarus—whom he had seen often while they were both alive. Lazarus was different, to be sure; gone were the rags he had worn, and gone were the dogs that had licked his sores when he lay beside the rich man's garbage cans. Nevertheless, the rich man recognized his old neglected neighbor. Obviously, memory was intact.

He also recognized Abraham, whom he had never known in life. Centuries separated their appearances on earth. Abraham was just a name to him, but, as the Lord told the story, "in Hades . . . he . . . saw Abraham . . . So he called to him, 'Father Abraham, have pity on me' " (verse 24).

This immediate recognition in afterlife was anticipated in the scene on the Mount of Transfiguration, when the disciples saw and recognized Moses and Elijah. The Lord did not introduce them— "Moses, this is Peter; Peter meet Moses," etc. There was immediate recognition of those historic figures.

The Apostle Paul undoubtedly heard of that experience, and he may have been thinking of it when he wrote of the future as contrasted with the "now." "Now we see but a poor reflection," he admitted, "but then we shall see face to face. Now I know in part; then I shall know fully, even as I am fully known" (1 Corinthians 13:12). In Heaven we shall have our memories intact, and probably considerably improved over what they are now. We shall also have an added faculty—the ability to recognize people whom we never knew on Earth. In God's eternal home there will be no strangers.